CALCUTTA AND RURAL BENGAL

CALCUTTA AND RURAL BENGAL

A.N. BOSE

GYAN

Published by

Gyan Publishing House
5, Ansari Road
Daryaganj, New Delhi-110002
Phone: 011-47034999, 9811692060
E-mail: books@gyanbooks.com

Distribution Network
gyanbooks.com
India, USA, Canada, UK, Australia

ISBN: 978-93-7225-220-0 (PB)

2nd Impression 2025

Printed at: Gyan Press, Delhi.

CALCUTTA AND RURAL BENGAL
Author: A.N. BOSE

CALCUTTA AND RURAL BENGAL : SMALL SECTOR SYMBIOSIS

CALCUTTA AND RURAL BENGAL

SMALL SECTOR SYMBIOSIS

A study prepared for the International Labour Office within the framework of the World Employment Programme

A. N. BOSE

INDIA

PREFACE

THIS STUDY originated as a follow up to an earlier study by Harold Lubell on the development and employment prospects of the Calcutta metropolis.[1] Like the earlier one, this study was undertaken within the framework of the research programme on urbanisation and employment of the ILO's World Employment Programme. The urbanisation programme was financed in large part by a grant to the ILO from the Ministry of Economic Co-operation of the Federal Republic of Germany.

Though originally designed as a study of the informal sector in the Calcutta metropolis, the analysis was broadened to cover a much wider horizon primarily for a better understanding of the original subject itself. The study, as now presented, centres around the proposition that a basic structural change replacing the still contiuning semi-colonial relationship by a symbiotic one between the city and the countryside, between industry and agriculture is the primary pre-condition for solving the mounting crisis both in the metropolis as well as in the countryside. And it also emphasises the corollary that in the absence of such a relationship, development of mere physical infrastructure like roads, transportation facilities and water supply and even slum improvement will not only not solve the main problems of the metropolis or of the countryside, it may further aggravate them.

Those who helped the author most in developing the above proposition were the large number of slum dwellers in Calcutta city with whom he has been associated since the student days, and the poor peasants with whom he has more recently become associated, first as member-Secretary of the Jute Inquiry Commission and then as a member of the State Planning Board, Government of West Bengal, and now as the Executive Vice-Chairman of the West Bengal Comprehensive Area Development Corporation.

The author is grateful to the social workers of CUSCON, CMPO and CMDA who conducted the field investigation on

1. Harold Lubell : *Urban development and employment : The prospects for Calcutta*. Foreword by J. Tinbergen (Geneva, ILO, 1974).

informal sector units in some selected slum areas in the Calcutta metropolis reported on in the study. The expenses of the above field investigation were covered by the ILO.

A number of suggestions were received from Harold Lubell, Jean Mouly, Kalmann Schaefer, S.V. Sethuraman and Robert Young who participated in a seminar held at the ILO in Geneva in July 1974 on an earlier draft of the study. Though the suggestions were extremely useful in revising the earlier draft, the full responsibility for the contents of this book rests with the author alone.

CONTENTS

CHAPTER I

INTRODUCTION

1.1 SCOPE OF THE STUDY

THIS STUDY was originally intended to cover only the pattern of functioning of the industrial units in the Calcutta area slums with a view to identifying their employment potential as a follow up to an earlier ILO World Employment Programme study of the urban development and employment problems of Calcutta.[1] However, in the course of the study itself, it was necessary to get involved in an examination of the nature of the informal sector, a significant part of which consists of small units in general and the industrial units in slums in particular ; of the pattern of its linkage with the "formal" i.e. the organised sector, the dominant sector, of the Calcutta economy ; of the nature of crisis of this organised sector leading to stagnation or even decline in employment ; of the impact of the latter on the informal sector, and then, of the steps to be taken to utilise in practice the productive employment potential of the informal sector.

This study, therefore, is concerned with analysing the pattern of existence and movement of the over-all framework of the economy of metropolitan Calcutta since it is only in relation to the latter that the specific role of one of its constituents, viz. the slum industries in the Calcutta area, can be properly understood. It should, however, be made clear that this short study cannot by its very nature go into a detailed investigation of the functioning of the whole metropolitan economy. It attempts to analyse some broad facts and to develop a hypothesis regarding the present over-all structure of the metropolitan economy. This hypothesis may be tested, through more elaborate effort, in some subsequent studies.

The central hypothesis of this study is that the informal and

1. Harold Lubell : *Urban development and employment : The prospects for Calcutta*. Foreword by J. Tinbergen (Geneva ILO, 1974).

the formal sectors operate in basically two different markets, that it is this that mainly differentiates the informal from the formal sector, and that these two sectors are dependent upon one another in much the same way that a colonial economy and a metropolitan economy are dependent upon each other. This means that the underdevelopment and backwardness of the informal sector are necessary conditions for the development and advancement of the organised, formal sector dominated by a few oligopolistic houses. That is why a basic change in the condition of the informal sector is dependent upon effecting a corresponding basic change in the mode of operation of the formal sector. An elaboration of this basic hypothesis is the main content of this study.

The above hypothesis has been complemented by another one which may be stated as follows : The current crisis in the metropolitan economy is a necessary consequence of its own structure and its nature of functioning. Although based on low productivity agriculture which supplies it with food and the most essential industrial raw materials, the metropolitan economy practically never produced any input which could have been used to improve the agricultural production base. The structure of the metropolitan economy was oriented towards making profit through export of goods (jute goods, tea, etc.) and in making purchases of agricultural raw material (raw jute, etc.) on the one hand, and provision of equipment, and of its repair and servicing for the transportation sector (railway wagons, heavy structurals for bridges, etc.) on the other. Up to the early 1950s, jute milling along with its associated activities was the dominant economic activity in the Calcutta metropolis. Since the middle of the 1950s, this dominance is being shared by the transport equipment centred engineering industry. None of these goods, in the main, is needed in the rural sector for increasing agricultural productivity. The metropolitan economy, based on that industrial structure, functions by imposing what may be called a different sort of market on the unorganised peasant economy—the main informal sector in India—whose poverty, hunger and backwardness guarantee that the organised metropolitan economy gets the food and the raw materials it needs. This "different market" is characterised by high rents (50 per cent of the gross produce), usurious interest rates (often exceeding 100 per cent per annum), very low wage and only seasonal employment, very low prices for the peasants' produce (although the same produce is sold to the ultimate consumer at high prices). The basis for the existence of this "different market" is provided by acute and increasing concentration of land holdings (and hence, of landlessness) and absence of employment opportunities in the non-agricultural sector. It is these characteristics of the market that force, say, a landless agricultural worker to work at a wage of less than Rs. 4 per man-day and that too for only half of the year and so remain hungry for most of the year ; similarly, it forces a small sharecropper to part with 50 per cent of his gross produce to the landowner which he would have consumed himself had he not been subjected to the forces in this "different" market. Similarly, an indebted poor peasant hands over a major part of his produce to the money lender to settle his usurious debt burden. The produce thus obtained from rent payment or debt repayment or enforcing a wage much below the minimum subsistence level, then becomes ths marketable surplus of which a major part ultimately finds its way to the metropolis for sustaining its economy. The economic force which sustains the metropolitan economy is thus based on keeping the poor peasants and sharecroppers hungry and backward. This is the essence of the current pattern of functioning of the metropolitan economy and the pattern it imposes on rural-urban relations. This same "backwardness" of the rural economy, however, is characterised by a low average level of productivity per hectare and very wide fluctuations in productivity. The low productivity causes the sluggishness in the rate of growth and the wide fluctuations force the sluggish economy into crisis. The wide fluctuation in productivity creates the basis for speculative commerce and this in its turn accentuates further the fluctuation in supply through hoarding. The current crisis of the sluggish metropolitan economy is, thus, inherent in its present structure.

The basic *way out* of this crisis-ridden sluggishness of the metropolitan and state economy lies in reorienting and changing the metropolitan industrial structure in such a way that it may provide the rural, agricultural sector with the inputs required to implement the current technological possibility of achieving a dramatic increase in productivity and a drastic reduction in the fluctuations in productivity in the agricultural sector. Such a restructured metropolitan eeonomy will then be able to sustain and draw in its turn its own sustenance from a restructured rural, agricultural sector. This is the mechanism which can put an end to the present pattern of relationship between the dominant Calcutta metropolis and its dominated rural and semi-rural hinterland. It is within this broad framework of a basic change in the relation between the most important constituents of the formal and the informal sector that we are to assess the present position and the changes required in the functioning of the informal sector within the Calcutta metropolis.

An attempt has also been made to demonstrate how the informal sector tries, may be in a distorted fashion, to restore the capital and labour intensities for our whole economy to a level which is desirable and relevant for utilising, in an optimal fashion, the current resource endowments in our labour surplus, capital scarce, backward country. It is not the smallness as such that makes a unit belong to the informal sector and so remain backward ; a small unit, which may otherwise be highly efficient, is now forced to remain outside the organised capital and commodity market, by the operation of a particular pattern of economy now in operation in our country, and thus become a victim of the unorganised "different" market which conspires to keep it backward and informal. An elaboration of this point will constitute an important part of our study.

1.2. Data base

The major data base for the study has been provided by the All-India Census for 1961 and 1971, studies of small-scale indusry carried out by the Bureau of Applied Economics and Statistics (formerly, State Statistical Bureau) in 1954, 1965/66 and 1971, a comprehensive survey of industries of the Calcutta Metropolitan District (CMD) carried out by the Calcutta

Metropolitan Planning Organisation (CMPO) in 1962/63, the study of small engineering units at Howrah by Jadavpur University in 1961, and the survey of the slum industries specifically carried out for the purpose of this study in 1974. The survey design and the questionnaire for the last survey have been presented in Annex I.

The different statistical surveys mentioned above are not comparable to each other either in coverage or in scope. Despite this, it should be possible to discuss a general trend regarding the pattern of change over the last fateful decade in our economy in general and in the informal sector in the Calcutta area in particular.

These statistical surveys by their very nature cannot often bring to the fore certain qualitative characteristics of the economy which may be crucial for understanding its basic nature. For example, official studies by the Government generally cannot take into cognisance the existence of a black market price or an illegal usurious rate of interest which may often be the most dominating feature of the economy under discussion. These defects of the official studies can to some extent be rectified by undertaking type studies to be carried out by investigators in those units which may have absolute confidence in the integrity of the investigator that these data will not be used in any way against the informant. These type studies, by their very nature, are extremely time consuming and cannot be undertaken by each and every investigator.

Accordingly, we were able to undertake only a few type studies, which did throw up some extremely valuable information particularly regarding the qualitative aspect of the problem under discussion, unravelling the specific mode of operation of the relationship between informal-sector and formal-sector units. These type studies are, therefore, another important data source for this study.

Analogous to the above-mentioned type tudy is the information thrown up in the discussions we held with responsible administrators, technocrats and other relevant persons with extensive knowledge in the field under study. This is, thus, also another source of "data" for this report. For obvious reasons, the exact sources of these "data" as well as those emanating from the type study, cannot be cited.

While analysing the data collected it was felt that for developing a correct understanding of the situation under study, and, what is often more important, for presenting that understanding in a universally acceptable and convincing form, it is necessary to generate a large mass of a new type of data. These data will include information relating to the nature of the bonds between the formal and the informal sectors, the mechanism of utilising the backward labour-intensive informal sector including the rural, agricultural sector as a whole for generating excessive profits for the metropolitan oligopolies—which are mainly commercial rather than industrial in character. Access to such data, by their very nature can be had most successfully primarily as a part of an endeavour to change the present situation. A small manufacturing unit or a poor peasant can discuss freely the rate at which he had to borrow money or the price at which he had to purchase inputs from (or to sell his output to) the influential trader of the area, only when he can be assured that he will no longer have to depend on that influential man and that he will get cheap credit in future from the banks, that his illegal usurious debt burden will be abolished, that he will get at least the same marketing facility which is now enjoyed only by the organised, formal sector, etc. A truthful data-based analysis of the informal sector can be facilitated enormously only when this analysis is linked up with a decisive attempt to change the situation which perpetuates the present backward condition of the informal sector.

Against the above background it may perhaps be appreciated why at least a part of this study could not have a sufficient data base and so why at least a part of the analysis had to content itself with only suggesting several hypotheses.

It may be mentioned that another study designed to develop an industrial development plan for West Bengal, which is to a large extent a follow-up of this present study, has been planned jointly by the members of the State Planning Board, the Indian Statistical Institute, and the Indian Institute of Management, in collaboration with several other local government and voluntary organisations. The component studies for developing this Industrial Plan will include : (a) a study of the industry mix required for meeting the basic needs of the people relating to food, clothing and shelter ; (b) study of the relations of production and exchange within and between large, medium and small-scale industries, as well as that between the industry sector and the other sectors of the economy in general and agriculture in particular ; (c) a study of selected Calcutta slum area industrial complexes for designing area specific development plans ; (d) a study of the major mineral resources of the area, viz., coal, with a view to developing a coal industrial complex ; (e) a study of the appropriate technology to be adopted in the different subsectors of industry, given the industry mix ; and (f) a study of the appropriate locations of industrial units, given the industry mix. The plan of this follow up study, however, has not yet been implemented.

CHAPTER II

COVERAGE OF THE INFORMAL SECTOR IN THE CALCUTTA AREA

2.1. COVERAGE : MANUFACTURING SECTOR

THE LATEST All India Census reveals the sector of employment of the people residing in Calcutta city in 1971. The sector divisions in the table next page are self-explanatory, except for "Household industry" (col. 3). The latter is composed of those industrial units which are conducted mainly by the members of the household, within the premises where the household lives, if in urban areas, and with an employment lower than 10, if using power. In 1971, there were 3,148,746 persons living in Calcutta city with an area of only 104 sq. km. Of these people, 37.0% were in the working force. This working force participation rate for Calcutta city is significantly higher than the corresponding state average of only 27.9%.

The table also shows the sector of employment of the people working in Calcutta city. Some of these workers do not reside in the city of Calcutta, just as some of the workers living in Calcutta do not work in any establishment situated in Calcutta city. While 0. 946 million persons worked in some establishments situated in Calcutta city, 1.166 million workers resided in the city in 1971. Thus a net 220,000 persons resided in Calcutta but worked in places outside the city limits. It is evident that of the above seven categories of workers, the more important categories from the point of view of employment are : trade and commerce, non-household industries, and other services including government offices. Of these three categories, attention in this report will be concentrated mainly on the industry sector, not only because this is the dominant directly productive sector of the metropolitan economy, but also because the central action required to be taken to rescue the economy from sluggishness will be with regard to this sector of the economy, as we shall see later. However, some attempt will also be made

TABLE 1

Sector of employment of workers living in Calcutta city and of persons working in Calcutta city, 1971

Item	Primary sector	Secondary sector			Tertiary sector			Total
	(agriculture and allied, and mining)	Household industry	Non-household industry	Construction	Trade and commerce, finance, banking and insurance	Transport, storage and communication	Public utilities,[a] public administration and other services	
1	2	3	4	5	6	7	8	9
A. *Workers living in Calcutta city, by sector :*								
Number	5746	7710	316149	28121	337845	158103	311868	1165542
Per cent	0.49	0.66	27.12	2.41	28.99	13 57	26.76	100.00
B. *Persons working in Calcutta city, by sector :*								
Number	4109	8468	318987	2428	338199	56508	216993	945692
Per cent	0.43	0.90	33.73	0.26	35.76	5.98	22.94	100.00
C. *Establishments in Calcutta city, by sector :*								
Number	680	2859	36245	60	69666	4565	13884	127959

Source : Census of India, 1971, Series 22 : West Bengal, Part II A, General Population tables and Part IIIA, Establishment tables (October 1974).

a. Electricity, gas and water.

to deal with other sectors, particularly the trade and commerce sector.

The total employment in the industrial units situated in the city of Calcutta, subdivided by major industry groups and employment size classes is presented in reference table A, a summary of which is given in table 2 next page. From the point of view of statistical compilation of data, the entire manufac turing industry in India is divided into the following groups ;

I. *Registered factory sector, composed of two sub-groups* :

(a) Census sector units : These are the industrial units employing 50 or more persons, if using power, and those employing 100 or more persons. All these units are covered by an annual census undertaken under a Central Act. Exhaustive statistical data relating to these units are available with a time lag of about five years.

(b) Sample sector units : These are the units employing between 10 and 19 persons if using power, and 20 to 99 persons, if not using power. These units are also surveyed annually but only through a sample.

II. *Non-registered factory sector, also composed of two groups :*

(a) *Non-household units* : This group is the main constituent of small-scale, handicraft and cottage industries operating mostly in an unorganised fashion. Pending further discussion later, regarding the rationale of designation, this part of the manufacturing industry sector is proposed to be considered as the "informal" part of the industry sector.

(b) *Household units* : already defined. This part also belongs to the "informal" sector.

Apart from the statutory registration under a Central Act, there are several other voluntary registrations introduced by several government organisations. One of these latter is that introduced by the small-scale and cottage industry departments for registering with them all the small units using less than Rs. 750 thousand (and in some specified cases for ancillary units, Rs. one million in plant and machinery). These small units, thus, belong both to the informal sector and the formal sector

TABLE 2

Number of units and employment of the manufacturing units belonging to census sector, sample sector and the informal sector, Calcutta city, 1971

Item	Registered factory units (formal sector)			Non-registered units (informal sector)			Total (all sectors)
	Census sector	Sample sector	Total formal	House-hold units	Non-house-hold units	Total infor-mal	
No. of units	467	2 485	2 952	2 859	33 293	35 151	38 103
Employ-ment	145 235	50 997	194 232	8 468	124 755	133 223	327 455

Source : Reference table A.

as defined above. However, this registration, being voluntary in nature and being undertaken mainly by those who want some government help, covers only a very small part of the relevant universe. Thus, even in Calcutta city only 22,300 units have been registered with the Directorate of Cottage and Small-Scale Industry as small-scale units upto 31.3.1977.

2.2. *Coverage : trade and commerce*

From the point of view of employment, the trade and commerce sector is the third most important sector in the Calcutta city, after the manufacturing, public administration, and other services' sectors. Compared to an employment of 327,000 in manufacture, and 212,000 in public administration and other services, there were only 192,000 in trade and commerce in Calcutta in 1971.

With minor omissions almost the whole of this division is covered by an Act called the West Bengal Shops and Establishments Act, 1963. So far, 266, 371 units (up to September 1973) with an employment of 532, 664 persons have been registered under this Act in 205 places in West Bengal where it has been enforced. (Source : Labour Directorate, W. Bengal). This Act provides for some welfare measures relating to employees, such as hours of work, payment of wages, etc. No basic information relating to the functioning of these units is made available, at least on a regular basis. No regular censuses or sample surveys are conducted covering these units.

Thus, though the whole of the trade and commerce in Calcutta city may appear to be, from the point of view of the law, belonging to the formal sector, in actual practice at least the smaller ones amongst these, in the retail business sector in particular, do operate in an informal fashion. If it is assumed that all the units in the division employing up to four persons per unit belong to the informal sector, then we obtain the breakdown shown in Table 3.

TABLE 3

Division of the trade and commerce units between formal and informal sectors, Calcutta city, 1971

Item	Units employing up to 4 workers (informal sector)	Units employing 5 and more workers (formal sector)	Total
1. No. of units	49 746	9 479	59 225
2. Employment	103 279	88 358	191 637

Source : Reference table A.

Thus, nearly 54 per cent of total employment and 84 per cent of all trade and commerce units in Calcutta city may be said to belong to the informal sector.

The only survey covering the commercial establisments in the Calcutta area appears to be that conducted by the then Statistical Bureau, Government of West Bengal in 1962/63. As per that survey, the total number of trade and commerce units in Calcutta city in 1962 was 69, 796 ; the corresponding number in 1971 in table 3 is 57,225, i.e. less than what it was in 1962. This survey did not make a separate estimate for the corresponding employment in Calcutta city. It made an over-all estimate for employment per unit for the different categories of these units for the Calcutta metropolitan district as a whole. Details of this estimate are presented in reference Table B. A summary of this table is given in table 4 below.

TABLE 4

Trade and commerce units and their estimated employment in Calcutta city and in other areas of the Calcutta Metropolitan District (CMD) (as defined in 1962), 1962

Item	No. of units by class of activity		
	Wholesale trade	Retail trade	Total
(1)	(2)	(3)	(4)
1. No. of units at :			
(a) Calcutta	8 267	61 529	69 796
(b) Howrah	580	8 430	9 010
(c) Other CMD	991	49 442	50 433
Total CMD	9 838	119 401	129 239
2. Employment per unit in the CMD :			
(a) family labour	1.51	1.40	1.41
(b) hired labour	4.70	0.73	1.03
Total labour per unit	6.21	2.13	2.44
3. Total employment in CMD :			
(a) family labour	14 855	167 161	182 016
(b) hired labour	46 239	87 163	133 402
Total labour	61 094	254 324	315 418
4. Investment per unit in CMD (Rupees) :			
(a) fixed capital	3 768	1 039	1 247
(b) working capital (stock per day)	14 824	2 742	3 662
Total capital per unit	18 592	3 781	4 909

Source : Reference Table B.

It may be clear from table 4 that an average unit in retail trade is not only smaller in size so far as employment is concerned, compared to that in the wholesale trade, it is also dominated by family workers. The average employment is 2.13 per retail unit. The average retail unit can be conceived of as being composed of units with employment varying from one to four persons. The number of such units as per the 1971 census was 45,817 in Calcutta (see table 6).

From an operational point of view, the retail trading units having employment of less than 5 per unit, of whom more than 50 per cent are family workers, may be defined as informal sector units among the trade and commerce establishments. If we follow this definition then it will be found that the retail trading units dealing in coal (1,862 units in Calcutta and 3,925 units in the whole of CMD) and those dealing with "furnishing" (310 units in Calcutta and 320 units in the whole of CMD) do not belong to the informal sector (see reference table B). Leaving aside those units, Calcutta city had 59,357 units in the informal trade and commerce sector in 1962. The corresponding figure for the CMD as a whole was 115,156 and all these units together employed 243,617 persons.

One of the crucial differences in the operating results between the formal and informal sectors may be made clear with reference to the two main categories of trade viz. wholesale and retail. In the wholesale trade of the Calcutta meropolitan District as a whole, average investment per unit was Rs. 3,768 in fixed capital and Rs. 14,824 in working capital (value of stock in a day) making a total investment of Rs. 18,592 per unit. The corresponding figure for the retail trade was Rs. 1,039 plus Rs. 2,742, equalling Rs. 3,781 per unit. The basic difference between these two categories will become more clear if we take up the rate of return over the invested capital. For wholesale trade, total profit was Rs. 42,426 per unit after deducting the imputed wage of the family workers at the rate at which the paid workers in this category got wages. This profit represents a rate of return of 228 per cent on the total capital invested. In the retail trade, however, total profit per unit was only Rs. 545 after deducting the imputed wage of family workers at the rate at which paid workers in wholesale trade got wages (about Rs 173 per month). The profit, thus, is nominal in absolute value (it represents Rs 32 per month per family worker in the retail trade unit) and this means that the owners in retail trade earn an income which is nearly equal to that of the wage of hired workers in the wholesale trade. We shall find this characteristic recurring in the manufacturing field also. As regards rate of return over investment it was only 15 per cent compared to 228 per cent in the wholesale trade. This is also a distinguishing characteristic of the informal sector. The above information has been summarised in table 5 below.

TABLE 5

Rate of return and income from the retail and the wholesale trade in the CMD, 1962
(in Rs.)

Item	Wholesale trade	Retail trade
(1)	(2)	(3)
1. Investment per unit (total)	18 592	3 781
of which : (a) fixed capital	3 768	1 039
(b) working capital	14 824	2 742
2. Income per unit of the owner	45 570	3 490
3. Imputed wage of family worker per unit[(a)]	3 144	2 945
4. Profit per unit [(2)-(3)]	42 426	545
5. Wage per hired worker per year	2 082	823
6. Profit as percentage of investment	228%	15%

(a) This is calculated at a rate paid to hired workers in the wholesale trade.

It may be noted that the wage level in retail trades was very low and it was only 0.4 times the wage in the wholesale trade sector. Despite this extremely low wage, the average income of the family running the retail trade units, including the imputed wage of the family worker, was only about Rs 291 per month. Even this low income level, it may be remembered, was nearly three times as high as what is now called in India the poverty line. This income could be provided to the family owning and working in the unit with an investment of only Rs 1.775 per employed person (including family workers) and ensuring a profit of only 15 per cent on invested capital. So far as the hired workers were concerned, their annual wage was as low as Rs 823 per year in 1962. If 30 per cent of a family of five can get even such a wage, their total income would have been Rs 1,235 per year, or just above Rs 20 per capita per month at 1962 prices, which is considered the poverty line in India. The corresponding per capita per month income of the owner family was about Rs 58 or about three times that for their hired workers. What appears to be low income in comparison to that in the large unit or in the wholesale trade, may be considered a good income against the background of the over-all situation in West Bengal where 70 per cent of the people are estimated to be below the poverty line. The relatively small income difference of about 1 : 3 between the wage earner's family and the owner's family may also be noted. We shall have occasion to discuss these points in greater detail when dealing with the manufacturing sector.

It may be seen in reference table B that within each of the broad groups of the wholesale and retail trade sector, there was a wide difference in their various characteristics. Thus, in retail trade, the emolument per hired worker varied from Rs 506 per year in the "grains" shops to Rs 977 in "miscellaneous other shops." Similarly the income of the family owning the units varied from as low as Rs 1,230 per year in the metal trade to as high as Rs 6,460 in the coal trade followed by Rs 5,670 in the "other food" group.

Keeping in mind the above characteristics of the trade and commerce units, we may now look at reference table C giving subsectorwise figures for the different types of non-manufacturing activities relating to the number of units and their employment in the different subsectors of formal and informal sectors for Calcutta city in 1971. This has been compiled from 1971

TABLE 6

Number of units and employment of the major groups of non-manufacturing units belonging to the formal and informal sectors, Calcutta city, 1971

Non-manufacturing activity groups	Item	Total formal sector employing 5 or more workers	Informal sector units employing 1 to 4 workers: Total up to 4	2-4	1	Grand total
(1)	(2)	(3)	(4)	(5)	(6)	(7)
1. Trade and commerce	Units	9 479	49 746	32 932	16 814	59 225
(total)	Employment	88 358	103 279	86 465	16 814	191 637
(a) wholesale	Units	2 220	3 929	3 307	622	6 149
	Employment	23 597	10 234	9 612	622	33 831
(b) retail	Units	7 259	45 817	29 625	16 192	53 076
	Employment	64 761	93 045	76 853	16 192	157 806
2. Banking, insurance	Units	5 088	5 353	4 180	1 173	10 441
and finance	Employment	133 399	13 163	11 990	1 173	146 562
3. Transport, storage and	Units	1 178	3 387	1 594	1 793	4 565
communication	Employment	50 480	6 028	4 235	1 793	56 508

(Contd.)

TABLE 6 (Continued)

Number of units and employment of the major groups of non-manufacturing units belonging to the formal and informal sectors, Calcutta city, 1971

Non-manufacturing activity groups	Item	Total formal sector employing 5 or more workers	Informal sector units employing 1 to 4 workers			Grand total
			Total up to 4	2—4	1	
(1)	(2)	(3)	(4)	(5)	(6)	(7)
4. Public administration and other services	Units	4 195	9 445	5 980	3 465	13 640
	Employment	192 765	19 266	15 801	3 465	212 031
5. Construction	Units	42	17	11	6	59
	Employment	2 387	41	35	6	2 428
6. Other non-manufacturing activity[a]	Units	293	631	413	218	924
	Employment	7 713	1 359	1 141	218	9 072
Total non-manufacturing activity	Units	20 275	68 579	45 110	23 469	88 854
	Employment	475 102	143 136	119 667	23 469	618 238

Source : Reference Table C. *a.* Agriculture and allied, mining ; electricity, gas, and water.

census data. A summary of reference table C is given in table 6 which shows that the major part of the wholesale trading units also had less than five workers per unit ; these units constituted nearly 64 per cent of the total number of units in wholesale trade. Similarly, in retail trade, while 86 per cent of the retail

TABLE 7

Number of units and employment in manufacturing and non-manufacturing, formal and informal sectors, Calcutta city, 1971

Item	Number		
	Formal sector	Informal sector	Total
Units :			
Manufacturing	2 952	35 240	38 192
Non-manufacturing	20 275	68 579	88 854
Total	23 227	103 819	127 046
Employment :			
Manufacturing	203 232	124 223	327 455
Non-manufacturing	475 102	143 136	618 238
Total	678 334	267 359	945 693

Source : Tables 2 and 6.

trading units had in each less than five workers, they claimed less than 37 per cent of total employment in those units. It, therefore, seems that rather than concentrating on the type of trade, it will be more correct, in the absence of any other data, to concentrate on the size of unit, irrespective of the nature of activity. The same remark is true for all other non-manufacturing activities listed in the earlier table. We may, thus, conclude that in Calcutta city in 1971, as many as 68,579 units out of a total of 88,854 (or 77 per cent of the total non-manufacturing units) belonged to the informal sector, and these units employed

143,136 workers including family workers, out of total employment of 475,000 (or 30 per cent of the total) in this group.

Table 7 adds together the numbers for manufacturing and non-manufacturing. The total number of informal sector units in 1971 came to 103819 units (82 per cent of the total of 127046 units in Calcutta city) offering employment to 267359 persons (28 per cent of total employment of 945,692 in the city). Within manufacturing, the informal sector accounted for 32 per cent of employment. Manufacturing thus accounted for 46 per cent of total employment in the informal sector but only 30 per cent of total employment in the formal sector, an indication of the importance of the informal sector for goods production in Calcutta city.

CHAPTER III

A REVIEW OF PAST SURVEYS OF INFORMAL SECTOR INDUSTRY IN METROPOLITAN CALCUTTA

SINCE THE early 1950s a number of surveys dealing with all or with parts of informal sector manufacturing (industrial units not covered by the Factories Act) in metropolitan Calcutta have been carried out by various agencies : an economic survey of small industries in West Bengal covering 1952-1954 ; the 1961 Census of India ; a 1960/61 survey of small scale engineering units in Howrah ; a 1962/63 survey of manufacturing in the Calcutta Metropolitan District ; a 1965-66 economic survey of small industry in West Bengal ; a 1970/71 survey of non-registered manufacturing in urban West Bengal ; and a 1974 pilot survey of income and expenditure of families of workers in informal sector industries in Calcutta city. This chapter presents and discusses data from these surveys, most of whose details have not hitherto been publicly available.

3.1 ECONOMIC SURVEY OF SMALL INDUSTRIES, WEST BENGAL, 1952-1954

The economic survey of small industries, 1952-1954, was the first of its kind in West Bengal. It sought to find out the detailed characteristics of all the industrial units not covered by the Factories Act, the non-registered units which make up the "informal sector" as defined here. These units were divided into 100 types and a report for each of the districts of West Bengal was compiled and published. Two additional reports—one covering West Bengal as a whole and the other covering the Calcutta industrial area (excluding Calcutta city)—were also published.

In 1952-1954 there were, according to this survey, 395 456 manufacturing units including cottage industry units in the informal sector of West Bengal. Most of these units were evidently

TABLE 8

Distribution of informal sector industrial units in different areas of West Bengal, 1952-1954

Area	No. of units	Percentage distribution of units	Total employment (including family labour)	Percentage distribution of employment
(1)	(2)	(3)	(4)	(5)
1. Calcutta city	30 577	7.7	121 529	12.8
2. Calcutta industrial area (excluding Calcutta)	16 145	4.1	46 650	4.9
3. Other urban areas	25 894	6.6 }	779 876	82.3
4. Other rural areas	322 840	81.6 }		
Total : West Bengal	395 456	100.0	948 055	100.0

in the rural areas. The pattern of distribution of these units in different areas may be clear from table 8. It may be mentioned that the area defined as the "Calcutta industrial area" did contain a few rural areas, although predominantly it was composed of the urban areas contiguous to Calcutta city. Thus, Calcutta city proper claimed in 1952 only 7.7 per cent of the informal sector units employing 12.8 per cent of total employment in such units in West Bengal. If we confine our attention to the urban areas of West Bengal and assume that the whole of the Calcutta industrial area was urban, then Calcutta city claimed more over than 42 per cent of the informal industrial units in Urban West Bengal and certainly significantly more of the employment of such units.

In table 9 below, the characteristics of the units in Calcutta city are compared with those for West Bengal as a whole. The most glaring characteristics of the informal sector units becomes clear from row 9 of table 9 dealing with estimated value added and its breakdown between wage income and all non wage incomes lumped together as "surplus". For West Bengal as a whole these units together could not produce any surplus or profit ; in fact there was a net deficit of more than Rs 96 million which meant operationally that the family workers or working proprietors could not earn an income at a rate even equal to the wage they themselves gave to their hired workers. The imputed wage bill of the family worker calculated at the current rate for hired workers in these units (less than Rs 538 per year per worker for West Bengal as a whole ; less than Rs 764 for Calcutta by itself) was nearly Rs. 409 million ; but the total income of the working proprietors of the units, including the imputed wages of family labour, came to only Rs 312 million. The income per unit came to only Rs 789 per year ; this was equivalent to Rs 411 per year per family worker in these units, or about Rs 13 per capita per month for those families. These units could offer a wage of Rs 538 per year to an average hired worker ; assuming 1.5 such workers in the families of hired workers, this meant an estimated average per capita per month income for those families also of about Rs 13. What is significant about this estimated per capita income is not so much its very low magnitude but that this level, at the then price situation, was only slightly lower than what was latter officially defined as the poverty level in India. It may also be remembered that it was estimated that even in 1972, 70 per cent of the people of West Bengal were below the poverty line. It can, thus, safely be said that these informal sector units as a whole in West Bengal could maintain 948,000 workers and their dependents, which might come to more than 2,500,000 persons in 1952-1954, at least near the poverty level. And this could be done with total assets of only Rs 375 per worker. Considering the relatively huge volume of investment made in large industry, the role of these small units in the battle against poverty is significant.

The informal sector units in Calcutta city earned significantly higher incomes than those for West Bengal as a whole. What has been said above about the role of informal sector units as a whole in the formidable battle against poverty is, therefore, applicable with much more force to the Calcutta area units.

TABLE 9

Characteristics of the informal sector industrial units as a whole, Calcutta city and total West Bengal, 1952-1954
(Values in Rs '000)

Item	Calcutta city	Total W. Bengal	Calcutta city as percentage of total West Bengal
(1)	(2)	(3)	(4)
1. No. of units	30 577	395 456	7.7
2. Total employment (number)	121 529	948 055	12.8
(a) hired	72 798	187 874	38.7
(b) family labour	48 731	760 181	6.4
3. Total value of assets	157 340	355 253	43.4
4. Total wage	92 802	509 608	18.2
(a) for hired labour	55 590	100 988	55.0
(b) imputed wage for family labour	37 212	408 620	9.1
5. Value of inputs used	354 647	799 899	44.3
(a) raw material	345 894	770 579	44.9
(b) fuel, electricity, lubricant	8 753	29 320	29.8
6. Other costs	36 285	76 992	47.1
7. Total cost of production			
(a) including imputed wage of family labour	495 253	1 386 499	37.7

(Continued)

TABLE 9 (Contd.)

Characteristics of the informal sector industrial units as a whole, Calcutta city and total West Bengal, 1952-1954 (Values in Rs '000)

Item	Calcutta city	Total West Bengal	Calcutta city as percentage of total West Bengal
(1)	(2)	(3)	(4)
(b) excluding imputed wage of family labour	446 522	977 879	45.7
8. Total value of output	539 425	1 290 028	41.8
9. Total value added (8)—(5)—(6) of which :	148 493	413 137	35.9
(a) total wage (4)	92 802	509 608	18.2
(b) total surplus	+55 691	− 96 471	xx
10. Income of the working proprietor of the units (including imputed family wage)	92 903	312 149	29.8

Note : Area coverages of both Calcutta city and West Bengal were smaller in 1954 compared to what they are now. Tollygunj was not then part of Calcutta city. Similarly, Purulia District and a few other areas were then outside the state of West Bengal.

xx Not applicable.

Although Calcutta city claimed less than 8 per cent of the informal sector industrial units in West Bengal, its corresponding share was more than 43 per cent for assets in those industries ; the corresponding shares for total output and value added were about 42 per cent and 36 per cent respectively. What is more significant is that these units as a whole in Calcutta city did produce a positive net surplus—this is perhaps their most distinguishing characteristic. There were, however, a few industry groups even in Calcutta city which could not generate any net surplus.

In table 10, the estimated values of those variables *per unit* have been presented separately for Calcutta city and for the state of West Bengal as a whole. This table brings to the fore the specific characteristics which distinguished Calcutta city units from the rest of the members of the same family in West Bengal. The first difference is in the composition of the labour force. While in West Bengal as a whole, only 20 per cent of the workers were hired, the figure was as high as 60 per cent for Calcutta. Secondly, the value of assets per unit in Calcutta was more than 5.7 times that of the corresponding average for West Bengal as a whole. This was associated with output of goods by 5.4 times and of value added by 4.6 times than that for West Bengal as a whole. Thirdly, it was possible for the Calcutta units to produce a net surplus of Rs 3,038 per unit including imputed wages of family labour amounting to Rs 1,217 per unit. This is perhaps the outstanding characteristic of the Calcutta city units as already mentioned.

An income of Rs 3,038 per unit including the imputed wage income of family workers in the 30,577 informal sector industrial units in Calcutta city meant that this sector provided an income of more than Rs 50 per capita per month, which was more than three times the poverty level income at the then price level, to 30,577 proprietor families. In addition, it provided an income of Rs 19 per capita per month for 48,537 wage-earning families, assuming that 1.5 hired workers had come from each family. The latter income level was also higher than the then poverty level income. Thus, the Calcutta city informal sector industrial units could in 1952 keep about 79,000 families, or

TABLE 10

Value of the characteristics per establishment, informal industrial sector, West Bengal and Calcutta city 1952-1954

Item	Calcutta city	Total West Bengal
(1)	(2)	(3)
1. Employment per unit	3.97	2.40
(a) hired	2.38	0.48
(b) family	1.59	1.92
2. Value of assets per unit	Rs 5 146	898
3. Wage per hired labour per year	746	538
4. Inputs and allied costs per unit (total)	12 785	2 218
(a) raw material	11 312	1 949
(b) fuel, electricity, lubricant etc.	286	74
(c) others	1 187	195
5. Value of output per unit	17 641	3 262
6. Value added per unit	4 856	1 045
(a) wage for hired labour per unit	1 818	255
(b) imputed wage for family labour per unit	1 217	1 033
(e) surplus per unit	+1 821	−244
7. Income of the working proprietors per unit	3 038	789

TABLE

Characteristics per unit of the 10 most important

Industry Group	No. of units	Assets (Rs.)	Family labour (No.)	Hired labour (No.)	Wage for hired labour (Rs.)
		Characteristics per unit			
(1)	(2)	(3)	(4)	(5)	(6)
1. General and electrical machinery (29)	4 087	5 062	1.51	3.03	2 251
2. Tailoring and allied (50)	4 123	5 271	1.43	1.65	1 515
3. *Bidi* products (43A)	3 206	540	1.40	2.29	1 731
4. Sweets, chana bhaja, etc (3A)	3 012	1 139	1.63	1.90	1 129
5. Printing, bookbinding etc. (45)	1 566	14 240	1.58	4.39	3 460
6. Gold and silver ornaments (63A)	2 628	5 779	1.57	1.94	1 690
7. Wood prod., furniture (41)	1 876	5 366	1.69	2.80	2 336
8. Footwear and leather goods (30)	2 338	2 362	1.98	1.20	1 022
9. Hosiery and knitted goods (47)	329	25 256	1.68	5.56	4 521
10 Chemicals (21)	290	13 747	1.59	4.91	3 601

Note : Figures in the bracket in column 1 give the industry code number

Source : *Economic survey of small industries*, West Bengal, 1952-54, State

11

industries in the informal sector, Calcutta city, 1952

Input and other cost (Rs).			Characteristics per unit		Income of working proprietor		
Raw materials	Others	Total	Cost of produc-tion (Rs.)	Value of output (Rs,)	Total (Rs.)	Imputed wage of family labour (Rs.)	Value added (Rs,)
(7)	(8)	(9)	(10)	(11)	(12)	(13)	(14)
7 081	1 208	8 289	10 540	13 911	3 371	1 122	5 622
12 580	1 783	14 363	15 878	19 549	3 671	1 313	5 186
5 793	2 176	7 969	9 700	11 862	2 162	1 058	3 893
7 628	912	8 540	9 669	12 225	2 556	969	3 685
4 818	1 388	6 206	9 666	13 485	3 819	1 245	7 279
17 180	1 020	18 200	19 890	22 896	3 006	1 368	4 696
15 286	2 119	17 405	19 741	22 474	2 733	1 410	5 069
7 160	1 340	8 500	9 522	13 117	3 595	1 686	4 617
36 659	3 220	39 879	44 400	43 953	447	1 366	4 074
21 363	2 333	23 696	27 297	35 558	8 261	1 166	11 862

used for the survey.

Statistical Bureau, Government of West Bengal.

395,000 persons, above the povery line, with total assets of only Rs 1,295 per worker (including family worker).

Although the informal sector units had been grouped in about 100 industry types, only 10 such industry types claimed 77 per cent of the totality of informal sector industrial units in Calcutta city (and 76 per cent of the employment in such units. The relevant information on these 10 industry types is presented in table 11. This table shows, amongst other things, that while the absolute level of participation of family workers per unit was more or less similar in all the industry types—it varied in the range of 1.40 to 1.69 per unit—for hired workers per unit it varied relatively rather widely in the range of 1.20 to 5.56. Again, in all those 10 types—with the single exception of the footwear and leather goods industry—the number for family labour was less than that for hired labour. The assets per unit varied widely—it was as high as Rs 25,256 per unit (or Rs 4,542 per worker) in the hosiery and knitted goods industry while it was as low as only Rs 540 per unit (or only Rs 236 per worker) in the *bidi* (indigenous cigarette) industry. It is instructive to note that the relatively most capital-intensive hosiery industry was the only industry amongst the 10 which failed to generate a net surplus, i.e. it failed to provide an income to the working proprietors even at the rate they themselves provided to their hired workers. Value added per unit of capital (assets) invested in the hosiery industry came to only Rs. 0.16 which was a very low ratio even if we compare it with the corresponding ratios in the organised formal sector. It is suspected that the hosiery units must have been passing through a special crisis pulling down the quantum of output and income during the period of the survey. In contrast, the same ratio for the *bidi* industry was as high as 7.21. This clearly shows that what is lumped together as the informal is in its turn composed of widely different elements, each of which needs to be studied separately to arrive at a policy decision as to what concretely should be done to improve their functioning.

The relationship between the wage per hired worker and value added per worker in the above 10 industry types gives an interesting picture. The relevant data are presented in table 12 below.

TABLE 12

Wage, value added, and investment per worker and rate of value added per unit of investment in the 10 most important informal sector industry groups in Calcutta city, 1952
(Rs per year)

Industry group	Per worker			
	Wage	Value added	Investment (asset)	Value added per unit investment
(1)	(2)	(3)	(4)	(5)
1. General and electrical machinery	743	1 238	1 115	1.11
2. Tailoring and allied	918	1 684	1 711	0.98
3. *Bidi* products	756	1 055	146	7.23
4. Sweets, *chana bhaja* etc.	594	1 044	323	3.23
5. Printing, bookbinding etc.	788	1 219	2 385	0.51
6. Gold and silver ornaments	871	1 338	1 646	0.81
7. Woodware, furniture etc.	834	1 129	1 195	0.94
8. Footwear and leather goods	852	1 452	743	1.95
9. History aud knitted goods	813	563	3 488	0.16
10. Chemical industry	733	1 825	2 115	0.86

3.2. CENSUS OF 1961

The next important survey in this line was the Census of India, 1961, which threw up very important data on industrial activity relating to employment and power use. Table 13 has been constructed on the basis of census data for the city of Calcutta.

According to the 1961 census, there were about 24,000 informal sector industrial units in Calcutta for which employment figures were available. Assuming that the units for which

TABLE 13

Distribution of all manufacturing units between formal and informal sectors, Calcutta city, 1961

Sector	No. of units
Formal sector (units employing 10-19 with power, and 20 and above)	3 056
Informal sector (units employing 1-9 with power and 10-19 without power)	23 716
of which :	
10-19 persons without power	1 249
6-9 persons	4 401
2-5 persons	15 161
1 person	2 905
Grand total	26 772

Note : This distribution excludes 6,165 units whose employment figures were not available.

employment data were not available were small units in the informal sector, then the total number of such units came to about 30,000. This tallies rather closely with the estimates made by the earlier survey on the number of such units in Calcutta in 1952 (table 8). It may, however, be remembered in this connection that while Tollygunj was not a part of Calcutta city in 1952, it was so in 1961. It, thus, appears that during the period from 1952 to 1961, the net number of informal sector units did perhaps contract to some extent. It may be remembered that the 1971 census revealed that the number of such units in Calcutta city was about 35,000 (see table 2 in chapter 2 and reference table A), denoting some net expansion during 1961-1971. Details of the 1961 data are given in reference table D.

Estimated total employment in the informal sector units in 1961, assuming that the unspecified units without employment data belonged to the modal informal subsector with employment of 2-5 persons per unit, was about 128,000. This may be compared with corresponding 1952 data of 122,000 and 1971 census

TABLE 14

Fluctuation in the number of units and employment in the informal sector and also in the formal sector, in six important industry groups in Calcutta city, 1961-1971

Industry group	Informal sector				Employment in the formal sector (in '000)	
	No of units		Employment (in '000)			
	1961	1971	1961 (Est.)	1971	1961 (Est.)	1971
(1)	(2)	(3)	(4)	(5)	(6)	(7)
1. Food industry	2 741	3 834	12	13	10	13
2. Miscellaneous textiles including tailoring	4 791	5 497	19	18	10	7
3. Wood and wood products	2 610	2 545	16	11	10	5
4. Paper, paper products, printing, publishing etc.	2 465	3 469	16	14	17	17
5. Leather and leather products	2 089	2 114	12	11	3	5
6. Metal products except machinery	2 778	2 715	12	11	30	13
A. Total six groups	17 474	20 174	81	78	80	60
B. Total all groups	23 716	35 240	128	124	111	203

Source : Census, 1961, 1971

data of 124,000. Almost stagnant figures of employment showing only a very marginal net average increase in employment, of about 100 persons per year over 19 years, seem to characterise the informal sector units in Calcutta city.

This small net increase in employment was, however, a resultant of very high mortality rates along with equally high birth rates amongst the small units. This aspect has to some extent been unravelled in the next section of this report covering the Calcutta Metropolitan Planning Organisation (CMPO) survey of industrial units in the Calcutta metropolitan district.

Comparing reference tables A and D gives some idea about the quantum of fluctuation in the number of units in the different industry groups and size classes. The relevant data regarding the six most important industry groups, from the point of view of 1971 employment data, in the informal sector in Calcutta city are presented in table 14. Despite some minor changes in the pattern of grouping of industrial establishments, the general trend of development of the informal sector during the period 1961-1971 may be seen from table 14. The trend is of general stagnation with even a marginal tendency to decline so far as the number of workers is concerned. Despite a fall in employment, there was a relatively big rise in the number of units denoting that during the 1961-1971 decade, the average size of the informal sector units became still smaller : it fell from an average of 4.6 persons per unit in 1961 to 3.9 in 1971. This trend of stagnation-cum-decline in employment was more marked for the formal sector where the fall in employment was substantial : from 80,000 in 1961 in those important industry groups 60,000 in 1971. This clearly brings to the fore the nature of the crisis in the metropolitan economy : the implementation in practice of the employment potential of informal sector industry in Calcutta city is integrally linked up with that of the formal sector, and, hence, is dependent upon a revival of the whole metropolitan economy.

As the 1961 census listing of all the industrial units in the Calcutta area was the population frame from which samples were drawn for the rather exhaustive sample survey conducted by the CMPO to be dealt with in detail in section 3.4

below, it is not necessary to go into further details about the 1961 census information as such here.

3.3. Survey of small engineering units in Howrah, 1960/61

The most intensive survey of its kind ever made in West Bengal was the survey of small engineering units in Howrah conducted by Jadavpur University with an interdisciplinary team of economists and engineers in 1960/61, supported financially by the Reserve Bank of India. Coverage of the survey was, however, extremely limited in terms of both industry and area. The survey dealt only with small-scale engineering units in Howrah city, the twin city of Calcutta on the other side of the river Hooghly. The reason for taking up this survey in this report is that it was only in this survey that an in-depth study was successfully made unravelling some of the essential characteristics of, perhaps, the most important group of informal industrial units in this area.

The survey report, published in 1964, was in two parts : the first part dealt with 200 of the larger amongst the small units employing 200 workers or more, the second dealt with 396 really smaller units employing 1-19 workers. Most of the latter units, as we shall see, employed less than 9 workers. We shall deal here with the second part of the report.

The composition of the sample of the smaller units was as follows :

Units employing		
(1)	10-19 persons	48 units
(2)	5-9 persons	191 units
(3)	4 or less persons	157 units
	Total	396 units

Of these 396 units, as many as 135 did job work executing orders as they came, 101 units manufactured machine parts, 33 were in machine manufacturing, 24 were manufacturing nuts and bolts and the remaining 137 units were distributed amongst 8 other groups.

That the typical ownership pattern of the small units is bound to be proprietary was clearly brought out by this survey. Out of 396 units, 277 were proprietary concerns, followed by 102 partnership units. Only 17 were registered as private limited companies. Thus, there was not a single unit which could utilise public subscription to capital.

The main reasons for the concentration of small engineering units at a particular locality of Howrah city were (i) the steady flow of customers who knew Howrah as an area where the most multifarious odd jobs could be got done at one or other of its units, (ii) the facility to start with only few machines, because other machine jobs could easily be arranged with neighbouring firms. The interdependence between the different units was a remarkable feature of Howrah engineering units. It was this characteristic which induced a skilled craftsman with some little capital to start a shop with the hope, seldom fulfilled, that some day his enterprise might become big.

The capital structure of these units is presented in table 15.

TABLE 15

Distribution of total capital of 396 units under different heads

Item	Total (in Rs 000)	Per unit (in Rs)
1. Fixed capital (depreciated book value) :		
(a) plant and machinery	4 630	11,692
(b) land and buildings	1 100	2,778
(c) furniture and fittings	200	505
Total fixed capital	5 930	14,975
2. Current assets :		
(a) loans and advances, outstanding credit	770	1,944
(b) cash in hand and with bank	530	1,338
(c) value of unsold products	520	1,313
(d) value of stock of raw materials	600	1,515
Total current assets	2 420	6,110
3. Total productive capital [(1)+(2)]	8 350	21,085

Relatively low fixed capital per unit (Rs 15,000) even in these engineering units may be noted : with about 6.2 workers per unit, only Rs 2,420 per worker. Another significant point to be noted is the very high proportion of current assets (or working capital) being blocked as "loans and advances" and outstanding credit (about 32 per cent of total) most of which was outstanding credit.

The problem of financing the units is illustrated by table 16. These data were based on information supplied by 92 amongst the above 396 small units which had shown some borrowing. It is apparent from the table that organised financial institutions

TABLE 16

Source of borrowing of the small engineering units, Howrah, 1961

Source	Total borrowing by 93 units	Borrowing per unit	Percentage distribution
(1)	(2)	(3)	(4)
1. Organised institutions (total) Rs	26 226	Rs 273	5.8
(a) commercial banks	1 950	20	0.4
(b) government and other public agencies	500	5	0.1
(c) co-operatives	23 776	248	5.3
2. Informal institutions (total)	424 688	4 424	94.2
(a) dealers	138 488	1 443	30.7
(b) relatives, partners and friends	106 600	1 110	23.6
(c) money-lenders	20 100	209	4.5
(d) not specific but mainly money-lenders	159 500	1 662	35.4
Total	450 914	4 697	100.0

played an insignificant role in providing finance to these small units and that this was one of the main characteristics of what we call the informal sector units. Organised financial institutions provided less than 6 per cent of the total finance made available to these units while informal institutions provided more than 94 per cent. The share of private money-lenders alone was as high as nearly 40 per cent of the total. The source of finance, as may be expected, was integrally linked up with the type of security offered for obtaining the loan. The pattern may be seen from table 17. By far the most important security that could be offered was "personal security." This also was an important characteristic feature of the informal sector and it was no wonder that with such security being the main type available, the main source of finance were personal friends, relatives and private money-lenders. Interest charged by money-lenders was about 36 per cent per year which was more than four times as high as the then prevailing rate from the organised institutional sector. This high interest rate, i.e. relatively high capital cost, is another distinguishing feature of the informal sector units. Thus, the capital market in which the small, informal units operate is qualitatively different from that in which the large formal sector units operate.

In spite of all these difficulties of finance, income of these units was relatively high. This may be seen from table 18 showing the breakdown of material input costs for the 292 profit-making units among the 396 small units. From the point of view of the owners, the total cost incurred came to : inputs (Rs 3,616,000) plus wages (Rs 2,259,000) plus rent and other items (interest etc.) (Rs 264,000) or Rs 6,142,000. Thus their income or profit came to : total output (Rs 12,250,000) less total cost (Rs 6,142,000) or Rs 6,108,000 which represented a return of nearly 49 per cent over total sales. This rate of return was indeed very high but even that high rate enabled the owners to earn, in absolute terms, an income of Rs 20,253 per unit per year or an income of only Rs. 1,688 per month. In this connection it may be remembered that this income represented not only profit but also, what in larger formal sector units would have appeared as, management cost, because proprietors of these units not only undertake the entire management work but also often do direct production work. The report commented on this point in a subsequent section that "the owner himself fulfils the functions of the manager including that of works manager and combining the duties of an industrial engineer, sales manager and supervisor, along with the responsibility of procuring finance which is by no means an easy job for a small man and he will take it as a bit hard on him if he is condemned as inefficient according to some text book definition of sound management. Most of them would have been doomed if they had attempted

TABLE 17

Borrowing classified according to type of security offered

	Type of security	Amount borrowed	Per cent to total
1.	Ornaments	Rs 19 850	4.4
2.	Landed property	3 000	0.7
3.	Machinery	7 788	1.7
4.	Life insurance policy	500	0.1
5.	Personal security	419 776	93.1
	Total	450 914	100.0

TABLE 18

Items of cost and income for 292 small engineering units earning profit

	Items	Amount ('000 of Rs.)
1.	Input costs (total)	3 619
	of which (a) raw materials	2 925
	(b) fuel, electricity and packing	344
	(c) tools and tool materials	350
2.	Value of total output	12 250
3.	Value added by manufacture [(2)−(1)]	8 631
	of which (a) wage	2 259
	(b) rent and other items	264
	(c) profit	6 108

anything of the sort contemplated in a text book of business management."

The remaining 104 units (which came to 26 per cent of the total number of units in the sample) did not show any profit. These were losing concerns. In this connection, the survey report stated that while in the larger units belonging to the formal sector, book-keeping losses were often due to failure to record all the items of income, the same is not, in the main, true for the informal sector units. Then the report stated : "The proportion of cases of genuine loss is somewhat higher among the smaller units than amongst the medium ones. Our investigation in the affairs in the second round revealed that in the first two or three years of its life, a unit is not at the height of its efficiency, and many of these small units are relatively new" (53 per cent were less than five years old). Secondly, the "very small ones often receive only a part, sometimes a particularly small part of the market value of their output". The last sentence reveals the most fundamental characteristics of the small units, i.e. they operate in a different market where the price of their output is very much less than what it would have been in the normal, organised formal sector market.

Another important characteristic of the small units was the amount of machine time they were forced to forego because they did not have sufficient orders owing to various causes. On a snap study, it was found that 730 machines out of a total of 2,107 (or 35 per cent) were idle. In addition, in a large number of cases the machines were working under-load.

This widespread non-utilisation of physical capital, on the one hand, and the often very meagre amount of physical capital provided per worker in the process of production, on the other, render misleading the widely-used statistical measures of labour productivity (output or value added divided by the number of workers) and the capital/output ratio (value of existing fixed capital divided by the value of output or value added) which is the inverse of capital productivity. A more sophisticated measure of these concepts, a production function, say, of the Cobb-Douglas type, is also normally not free from the defects which are evident in simple two-factor ratios, although the production function approach is conceptually more realistic because it explicitly takes into consideration the mutual interdependence between capital, labour and output.

Assuming linearity, i.e. constant marginal productivities for each of the two factors, capital and labour, and valuing capital at replacement cost, the report under study derived the following two production functions, one each for the medium and small units :

medium : $u = 1.90\,\overline{K}^{0.32}\,a^{0.68}$ with a correlation of 0.86

small : $u = 4.26\,\overline{K}^{0.51}\,a^{0.49}$ with a correlation of 0.85

where u = net value added by manufacture

$\overline{K}$ = value of capital at replacement cost

a = number of men employed

It may be noted in passing that though the production functions for medium units suggested that the share of labour in value added should have been, under competitive conditions, 68 per cent, in actual practice this share was less than half. This may be considered an inevitable situation in a labour surplus economy with extremely unorganised labour. Thus, even in the small units, the production function suggested that the labour should have received 49 per cent of value added, while the actual share of wage in value added was only 26 per cent. We shall refer to these production functions again while dealing with the next survey we are going to cover.

This section may be concluded by mentioning some other interesting characteristics of these small engineering units at Howrah :

(a) 62 per cent of owners were either skilled labourers or were in service before they started their respective units ;

(b) 77 per cent of owners belonged to the Howrah district itself ;

(c) 69 per cent of owners started their unit with their own savings ;

(d) 46 per cent of the units occupied less than 500 sq.ft. each and only 14 per cent occupied more than 2,500 sq. ft. per unit ;

(e) average HP per power using unit (358 units) was 6.23 ;

(f) 81 per cent of the machines used were Indian, of which 25 per cent were self-made ;

(g) 44 per cent of the units worked at less than full capacity and for 64 per cent of that was due to poor market demand ; and

(h) only 33 per cent of the units could sell their goods at market prices.

3.4. CMPO SURVEY OF 1963/64

The survey of manufacturing industry in the CMD conducted by the CMPO in 1962/63 is perhaps the only industry survey conducted so far, at least in the state of West Bengal, which took into account the different characteristics of all the industry types in all size classes, from the smallest to the largest, in one survey. It pertains, however, to a particular area—the Calcutta metropolitan district. Characteristics of the different strata and sub-strata can be compared with each other through the findings of this survey, but in a static framework with reference to the situation in a particular year. The analysis of the informal sector amongst the manufacturing units may usefully be strengthened with the data available through this survey.

The CMPO survey was based mainly on the population frame provided by the 1961 census. For the purpose of the survey, the population of the industrial units in the CMD was grouped under:

(i) 12 types of industries;

(ii) four employment size classes, with a further subdivision into four sub-groups of the smallest employment size class ; and

(iii) three sub-areas of the CMD, viz. Calcutta city, Howrah city and the remaining areas of the CMD.

Thus, there were $12 \times 4 \times 3 = 144$ strata for this survey.

For the purpose of the present discussion the most interesting groups were the employment size classes which were as follows:

A : units employing 100 persons or more ;

B : units employing 50 to 99 persons ;

C : units employing 25 to 49 persons ; and

D : units employing 1 to 24 persons.

The last group was further subdivided into :

D_1 : units employing 11—24 persons and using power ;

D_2 : units employing 1—10 persons and using power ;

D_3 : units employing 11—24 persons and not using power ; and

D_4 : units employing 1—10 persons and not using power.

In accordance with our definition of the informal sector, the units belonging to subsectors D_2, D_3 and D_4 may, with minor adjustments, be said to belong to the informal sector. The data from this survey can, then, be conveniently grouped under three heads :

(i) Large units belonging to groups A, B and C—all of which were covered under the Factories Act.

(ii) Medium units, also covered under the Factories Act and belonging to sub-group D_1.

The above two groups together, viz. $A+B+C+D_1$, may be said to constitute the formal sector.

(iii) Small units belonging to sub-groups D_2, D_3 and D_4. These together constituted the informal sector.

Almost all the data have been presented in the report for this survey for the four broad employment size classes and only some data have been presented with a further sub-division of the smallest size class. We therefore present here the data not only as per the regrouping suggested in the earlier paragraphs but also as per the four broad employment size classes. The latter will at least provide a trend of variation of a particular characteristic from a larger to the smaller-sized units and may provide us with sufficient insight as to its likely variation for the smaller-sized unit within the last size class.

Let us start presenting the results of the survey with a very interesting finding. In the course of conducting the sample survey in 1963, on the basis of samples selected from a population listing of 1961, it was found, amongst other things, that a large proportion of sample units, responsible for more than 10 per cent of total employment in CMD industries in 1961, "died" during the two years 1961/62-1962/1963. But this "death" was not equally distributed between the different size classes. This may be seen from table 19.

TABLE 19

Proportion of employment in each group lost due to death of units, 1961/62—1962/63 (Per cent)

Employment size class	Calcutta	Total CMD
(1)	(2)	(3)
A (100+)	0.8	3.1
B (50-99)	8.6	8.7
C (25-49)	9.4	9.5
D (1-24)	18.4	23.6
Total	11.6	10.5

It is clear from the above table that the smaller the size, the higher the probability of death, and looking at the big increase in the probability with the size class D, it can be surmised with sufficient confidence that the smaller amongst those in the size class D must be suffering from an even higher rate of mortality.

According to the census list (October, 1960,) there were 32,308 industrial units in Calcutta city of which 31,240 or 96.7 per cent of the total, belonged to the size class D and accounted for 54 per cent of total employment in industry. Thus, in numbers of units and employment, the predominant form of private enterprise, even in the city of Calcutta proper, was small enterprise belonging to the informal sector. Of the 7895 units closed down during 1961/62, about 98.9 per cent were small units. These 7809 closed small units constituted 25 per cent of all the small units existing in October 1960 in Calcutta city.

It may be clear from the above how mercilessly the economic system now existing in India is destroying the main form of private enterprise operating in the country. Private enterprise is being destroyed, not due to the operation of the public sector, but, as we shall see later, due to lack of operation or inefficient operation of the public sector. We shall argue later that a decisive and properly oriented intervention of the public sector, of the Government, is an essential pre-condition for saving small enterprise in the country. The relatively higher rate of mortality may, thus, be taken as the first important characteristic of the units in the informal sector.

Total employment in the industrial units in the CMD in 1961 was 904,000, of which 239,000 were in Calcutta city proper. Despite death of units during 1961/62—1962/63, the units which survived up to 1963 offered employment to 926,000 persons. This means that the units which survived expanded at a rate which could more than balance the loss in employment due to death of units. But this rate of expansion was not the same for all the employment size classes. The pattern may be seen from table 20.

TABLE 20

Employment by size class, 1961/62- -1962/63
(in '000 and per cent)

Employment size class	Calcutta 1961/62	Calcutta 1962/63	Calcutta % change	Total CMD 1961/62	Total CMD 1962/63	Total CMD % change
(1)	(2)	(3)	(4)	(5)	(6)	(7)
A (100+)	73.6	92.6	25.8	526.0	619.5	17.1
B (50–99)	16.3	17.4	6.7	35.9	34.1	— 5.0
C (25–49)	20.3	25.5	25.6	33.5	53.8	60.6
D (1–24)	129.1	93.8	−27.3	308.2	218.4	—29.1
Total	239.3	229.2	— 4.2	903.6	925.8	2.5

Combining the above two tables we find that, despite a loss of employment due to death of the unit by 3.1 per cent in the size class A in the CMD, there has been a net increase in employment in this size class *as a whole* by plus 17.1 per cent due to expansion of employment of the *remaining units.* This means that, in absolute terms, the large units in the CMD employed 526,000 persons in 1961 ; by 1963 some of these units employing about 16,000 (3.1 per cent of 1961 employment) died and the remaining units employing 510,000 in 1961 expanded by 1963 to an employment level of about 620,000 denoting a rate of expansion of employment by 21.6 per cent in two years or

10.8 per cent per year. The rates of expansion for the surviving units in the different size classes are presented in table 21.

TABLE 21

Rate of expansion of employment of the units existing in 1961 and surviving up to 1963, in the different size classes, Calcutta and CMD, 1961/62—1962/63 (in '000)

Employment size class	Calcutta			CMD		
	Employment		%	Employment		%
	1961	1963	change	1961	1963	change
(1)	(2)	(3)	(4)	(5)	(6)	(7)
A (100+)	73.0	92.6	26.8	509.7	619.5	21.5
B (50-99)	14.9	17.4	16.8	32.8	34.1	4.0
C (25-49)	18.4	25.5	38 6	30.3	53.8	77.6
D (1-24)	105.3	93.8	—10.9	235.5	218.4	— 7.3
Total	211.6	229.3	8.4	808.3	925.8	14.5

The columns depicting percentage change of employment in table 21 clearly demonstrate that the small units only, which showed a negative growth rate, must have been suffering from distinctly different maladies which did not haunt the large and medium units. This brings out the second most important characteristic of the informal sector units, viz. relative and absolute inability even for the surviving small units to expand themselves. We shall discuss later the great disadvantage from which these small units suffer. Against that background their inability to expand may appear in a different light, viz. the doggedness with which the small informal units were fighting for survival, because for them, it was literally a question of life and death. This doggedness born out of very grim reality, may be considered as the third important characterstic of the informal sector.

We may now take up a detailed study of the "survey universe" of industrial units in the Calcutta area which existed in 1961 and continued to exist in the same location up to 1962/63.

It was this survey universe which was stratified according to the design discussed earlier.

Table 22 presents the volume of employment in the formal and informal sectors, as we have defined them, separately from Calcutta city and the CMD as a whole covering the "survey universe".

TABLE 22

Volume of employment claimed by different sectors in the manufacturing industry in Calcutta and in CMD survey universe, 1962/63
(in '000)

Sector	Total employment		Percentage distribution of total employment	
	Calcutta	CMD	Calcutta	CMD
(1)	(2)	(3)	(4)	(5)
1. Formal sector (total) $(A+B+C+D_1$	176	788	76.9	85.1
(a) large units $(A+B+C)$	135	707	59.0	76.4
(b) medium units (D_1)	41	81	17.9	8.7
2. Informal sector (total)	53	138	23.1	14.9
(a) D_2 : 1-10 persons with power	17	26	7.4	2.8
(c) D_3 : 11-24 persons without power	19	69	8.3	7.5
(c) D_4 : 1-10 persons with power	17	43	7.4	4.6
3. Grand total	229	926	100.0	100.0

In studying table 22, as well as the others which will follow in this section, it should be remembered that these tables did not take into account the employment of the new units born during 1961/62–1962/63. Because the birth rate of new units in the small and informal sector, as we shall see later in a different section, is much higher than that in the medium and large units, the relative share of employment of the small and informal units in the totality of all the units existing in 1963, must have been higher than what may appear from the above table. Moreover, the small units which could survive at least two years are certainly relatively more "sturdy" and more efficient than the over-all average of the small units.

According to table 22, 23 per cent of industrial employment in the survey universe in Calcutta city and 15 per cent of that in the CMD as a whole was in the informal sector. A relatively higher concentration of informal sector units in Calcutta city may be noted.

In table 23 below, the more important characteristics of the industrial units in Calcutta city survey universe, as defined earlier, are presented. What may strike one as improbable in this table is the relatively high use of capital by the smaller units. If we start with what may be called perhaps the scarcest resource in the metropolis, viz. space, it is found that, on an average, the smallest sized units (size class D) used nearly twice as much space as was used by the largest sized units (size class A). It appears that smaller the size, the higher was the space per employee. The reason behind this higher rate of space use, and, as we shall see later, also of other elements of capital use, by the smaller units was not investigated in this survey, because when the survey was designed, no one expected such a result. The survey report advanced a hypothesis for explaining this phenomenon. It runs as follows : The higher space use per employee was a resultant of :

(a) absence of multiple shift working in small units ; while in many of the large units, 2-3 shifts per day was a normal phenomenon. Therefore, while the same space or machine could be used more than once by more than one worker in the different shifts in the larger units, this was not done in the smaller units. Thus while in "D" class units, 91 per cent of the total workers in that class belonged to single shift units, the corresponding proportions for the size classes A, B and C were respectively 36, 68 and 89 per cent.

(b) When a factory was started, expectation of its expan-

TABLE 23

Characteristics of the industrial units in the different employment size classes, survey universe, Calcutta City, 1962

Employment size class	Space per employee (sq. ft.)	Gross value added per 100 sq. ft. (Rs.)	% of units started during last 5 years	Volume of water used per day (in gallons)	% of units using power	Installed HP per employee in power using units	Estimated capital per employee (Rs.)		
							Equipment	Land and building	Working capital
(1)	(2)	(3)	(4)	(5)	(6)	(7)	(8)	(9)	(10)
A (100+)	216	2 290	28	35	87·2	0·89	1 992	1 481	6 090
B (50-99)	295	1 287	53	70	89·6	0·80	1 522	1 279	4 284
C (25-49)	519	770	35	50	71.7	1.00	1 016	1 121	2 806
D (1-24)	423	758	90	24	38.7	1.32	2 188	4 763	4 111
All units	340	1 188	85	35	41.2	1.02	1 928	2 768	4 779

sion played a role in deciding the amount of space earmarked for it. So far as the small units were concerned, as most of the units were new, their expectation of expansion either did not get time to be fulfilled or, worse, their average employment contracted over time. The opposite happened for the larger units. It may be remembered that during the two years 1961/62—1962/63, employment in small units decreased by 11 per cent while the same had increased by 17 to 39 per cent in the large and medium units. Owing to the time lag in changing the amount of space with the change (particularly when the change was in negative direction) in employment, space per worker was bound to be relatively high for smaller units.

(c) Knowledge of space planning must have been more deficient with the smaller units than for the larger ones and that also might have led to an inefficient, high space use for small units.

(d) The industries requiring relatively larger space might have accounted for a relatively larger proportion of small units. Thus, the industry with the highest amount of space per worker (1,037 sq. ft.), viz. food, claimed 47 per cent of its employment in the small units ; the industry with second highest space per worker (763 sq. ft.), viz. miscellaneous other industry, claimed 89 per cent of its employment in the small units. On the other hand, the industry with the smallest amount of space per worker (128 sq. ft), viz. printing, claimed only 40 per cent of its workers in the small units. Again, the industry with second lowest amount of space per worker (224 sq. ft.), viz. engineering, claimed only 32 per cent of its workers in its small units.

What has been said above about the reason behind the relatively higher amount of space use in small units is also applicable with regard to use of other fixed assets. An added factor in pushing up the money value of, particularly, land and building for the small units was the relatively much higher rent it had to pay for the space it rented. This high rent became reflected in higher capitalised value of land and building. The small units, by their very nature, want to remain as near to the centre of demand as possible. It was necessary for the type of business they did and also because their daily production was not sufficient to engage regularly any unit of modern transportation (lorry, railway wagon etc.). They have to depend on what may be called informal sector transportation, such as push carts, rickshaws or even just a "coolie". The vital role this informal sector transportation plays in enabling the small industrial units to function in and around the metropolis is very often lost sight of. The rent cost for the small units is also high because relatively a far larger number of these units were new and hence had to pay higher rent, while the older units often paid rent at a lower rate, contracted earlier. Moreover, the proportion of units in rented sheds was far higher for the smaller units, as indicated in table 24.

TABLE 24

Proportion of rented units amongst new and old units in the different size classes, survey universe, Calcutta city, 1962
(Per cent)

Employment size class	Proportion of rented units amongst		
	"Old" units started before 1956	"New" units started during or after 1956	All combined
A (100+)	77.9	56.8	71.1
B (50-99)	91.8	84.3	89.2
C (25-49)	79.8	96.5	84.1
D (1-24)	97.7	97.5	95.5
All Combined	92.4	97.6	94.8

Remembering what has been stated above, we may now go back to table 23. It is clear from that table that while fixed capital (equipment plus land and buildings) per employee in the small units in size class D was as high as Rs 6,951 per employee, it was almost exactly half of that (Rs 3,473) for the larger units in size class A. Thus, in the Calcutta area in 1962, the small units were significantly more capital intensive compared to the large units. An additional reason for the higher capital intensity for the smaller units arose because in calculating the value of fixed capital, its depreciated book value was taken into account. This made the value of fixed capital relatively higher for the small units because most of those units were relatively new.

That the phenomenon of higher capital intensity for small units was not peculiar to Calcutta city, but was also prevalent, though not to the same extent, in the other areas of the Calcutta metropolitan district as well, is evident from table 25.

TABLE 25

Fixed capital per employee in different size classes in the different areas of CMD survey universe, 1962
(in Rs.)

Area	Fixed capital per employee in the size class			
	A	B and C	D	Total
(1)	(2)	(3)	(4)	(5)
1. Calcutta city	3 473	2 407	6 951	4 696
2. Howrah city	3 575	1 956	2 840	3 204
3. Other areas of CMD	3 623	4 293	2 597	3 483
Total CMD	3 597	3 105	4 485	3 760

This phenomenon of higher capital intensity for small units is being emphasised here not only because it is contrary to widely held belief, but also, and mainly, because it is necessary to point out that this higher intensity was due not so much to technological reasons, but to the socio-economic institutional factors. We shall take up this issue in a later chapter and also in the discussion of capital productivity below.

How the small units are handicapped by lack of finance may be clear from table 26 showing the volume of working capital per employee.

It may be seen that for the CMD as a whole, an average small unit could get hold of less than half of the working capital per employee compared to what could be obtained by the large and medium units. And that was despite the fact that value of

TABLE 26

Working capital per employee in the different size classes in the different areas of CMD, 1962
(in Rs.)

Area	Amount of working capital per employee in size class			
	A	B and C	D	Total
(1)	(2)	(3)	(4)	(5)
1. Calcutta city	6 091	3 406	4 111	4 779
2. Howrah city	5 795	4 129	1 208	4 583
3. Other areas of CMD	5 022	7 621	1 282	4 517
Total CMD	5 245	5 165	2 492	4 588

input per unit of output in the small units, in all the areas of CMD, was actually higher than those for larger units, indicating higher need for working capital for smaller units. It is no wonder, therefore, that output and value added per worker or per unit of fixed capital would tend to be relatively lower for smaller units.

Gross value added (i.e. value added including depreciation) per employee, as expected, was much lower in the small units compared to the larger ones. But the wage level was not lower in the small units to the same extent, and that further reduced non-wage income or surplus per employee in the smaller units. The relevant data for gross value added and gross surplus (i.e. gross value added minus wage) per employee are presented in table 27.

In a labour-surplus, capital-scarce country like India, a more relevant measurs of efficiency is value added and surplus per unit of capital invested, rather than per unit of labour. Such an estimate is presented in table 28. It may be seen from table 28 that while in Calcutta city proper, the small units appeared to be suffering from low capital productivity, the situation in other areas, particularly in Howrah, was favourable for the small units. Taking the CMD as a whole, despite the innumerable difficulties the small units had to face, capital productivity in

TABLE 27

Gross value added (GVA) and Gross surplus (GS) per employee in different size classes in the different areas of CMD, 1962 (in Rs.)

Area	Item	Amount per employee in the size class A	B	C	D	Total
(1)	(2)	(3)	(4)	(5)	(6)	(7)
1. Calcutta	GVA	4 940	3 800	4 002	3 205	4 040
	GS	3 352	2 720	2 200	2 221	2 794
2. Howrah	GVA	3 700	4 200	3 300	2 200	3 400
	GS	2 100	2 700	2 200	1 000	1 900
3. Other areas	GVA	4 130	2 984	2 844	1 593	3 618
	GS	2 763	2 006	2 036	711	2 363
Total CMD	GVA	4 212	3 526	3 444	2 331	3 699
	GS	2 794	2 446	2 475	1 377	2 429

small units was not very much lower compared to the large and medium units.

Of the various difficulties of the small units, if we can remove only one, viz. constraints to utilisation of full capacity, then we may be able to discover the real technological position of the small units vis-a-vis the larger ones. In my doctoral dissertation prepared under the guidance of Prof. J. Tinbergen (*Implications of capacity utilisation : A study of the Calcutta Metropolitan District*), it was shown that taking the CMD as a whole, the space per worker for small units employing 5-24 workers, could be reduced from 740 sq. ft. to 190 sq. ft. if these units could use their full production capacity. The corresponding reduction for the large units employing 100 or more workers would be from 510 to 210 sq.ft. only. Similarly, with full capacity utilisation, value of machinery per worker could be reduced from Rs 1,762 to Rs 451 in those small units ; for large units, the corresponding reduction would be from Rs 2,057 to Rs 861. With respect to capital productivity also, it was shown that book value of plant and equipment per Rs 1,000 gross value added could be reduced from Rs 775 to Rs 199 for small units, the

TABLE 28

Gross value added (GVA) per Rs. 1,000 of plant and machinery and also per Rs. 1,000 of productive capital (PC) in different size classes in the different areas of CMD, 1962

(in Rs.)

Area	Item	Amount in size class				
		A	B	C	D	Total
1. Calcutta	(a) GVA per Rs 1,000 of plant	2 480	2 495	3 936	1 465	2 095
	(b) GVA per Rs 1,000 of PC	517	537	809	290	426
2. Howrah	(a) GVA per Rs 1,000 of plant	1 109	2 709	3 217	1 864	1 299
	(b) GVA per Rs 1,000 of PC	390	434	776	540	428
3. Other areas of CMD	(a) GVA per Rs 1,C00 of plant	2 027	2 183	2 512	1 828	2 024
	(b) GVA per Rs 1,000 of PC	478	370	199	411	452
Total CMD	(a) GVA per Rs 1,000 of plant	1 975	2 404	3 241	1 5 99	1 960
	(b) GVA per Rs 1,000 of PC	476	456	400	334	443

TABLE 29

Plant characteristics for large and small units in the CMD at actually realised levels of capacity use and at potential full capacity

Size class in the CMD	Space per worker (sq. ft.)		Machinery per worker (Rs)		Machinery per Rs 1,000 value added (Rs)		Space required for Rs 1,000 value added (sq. ft.)	
	Actual	Potential	Actual	Potential	Actual	Potential	Actual	Potential
(1)	(2)	(3)	(4)	(5)	(6)	(7)	(8)	(9)
1. Large units employing 100 or more workers	510	210	2 057	861	456	187	111	37
2. Small units employing 5 to 24 workers	740	190	1 762	451	775	199	323	106
Difference [(1) less (2)]	—230	20	295	410	—319	—12	—212	—69

corresponding reduction for the large units would be from Rs 456 to Rs 187. The above data are summarised in table 29. With full capacity utilisation, the small units would be at least as efficient as the large units, not only from the point of view of generating employment per unit capital, but also from that of generating income or value added per unit capital.

The gap between employment and income actually realised and the potential at full capacity as estimated for the above study is shown in table 30. The inability to utilise the already existing and installed production and employment capacity resulted in depriving the then Calcutta area of an additional income of nearly Rs 6,700 million (or an additional income of more than Rs 1,000 per capita per year for the people of that area) and of an additional productive employment of 1.6 million (the level of unemployment in the then CMD was less than 0.6 million.)

TABLE 30

Estimated level of income and employment in different size classes of CMD industries and their corresponding full capacity potential, 1962

	Volume of income (Rs. million)		Volume of employment ('000)	
Employment size class	Actual 1962	Full capacity potential	Actual 1962	Full capacity potential
1. Units employing 100 plus workers	2 790	7 343	619	1 478
2. Units employing 25 to 99 workers	354	1 276	88	317
3. Units employing 5 to 24 workers	434	1 691	191	746
Total units employing 5 and above workers	3 578	10 316	898	2 541

This section may be concluded with a brief reference to the differences in the various characteristics between the different sub-groups within the small units in size class D. As mentioned earlier, there were four sub-groups in this size class, viz : D_1 : units employing 11-24 persons and using power, D_2 : units employing 1-10 persons and using power, D_3 : units employing 11-24 persons and not using power, and D_4 : units employing 1-10 persons and not using power. It may be remembered that the D class units employed 94,000 persons in the Calcutta survey universe, and the total for the CMD as a whole was 219,000. The pattern of their distribution may be seen from table 31. Table 31 and Table 32 should be placed *before* we start re-section 3·5.

TABLE 31

Employment in the four different sub-groups of small units in size Class D, CMD survey Universe, 1962
(in '000)

Area	Total employment in the units in the sub-class				
	D1	D2	D3	D4	Total D
(1)	(2)	(3)	(4)	(5)	(6)
Calcutta city	41	17	19	e7	94
Howrah city	9	4	1	3	17
Other CMD	31	5	49	23	108
Total CMD	81	26	69	43	219
	(31.0%)	(11.9%)	(31.5%)	(19.6%)	(100.0%)

TABLE 32

Gross value added per employee in different sub-classes
(in Rs.)

Area	Gross value added per employee in the sub-class				
	D1	D2	D3	D4	Total D
(1)	(2)	(3)	(4)	(5)	(6)
Calcutta	4 700	2 600	3 000	1 200	3 200
Howarh	2 600	2 000	1 400	800	2 200
Other CMD	1 794	1 742	1 445	1 610	1 593
Total CMD	3 338	2 308	1 870	1 386	2 360

Table 32 presents the gross value added per employee in the different sub-classes of D-size class.

3.5 ECONOMIC SURVEY OF SMALL INDUSTRY, WEST BENGAL 1965/66

In 1965/66, the Bureau of Applied Economics and Statistics conducted a survey of non-registered industrial units (i.e. informal sector units). The main findings of this survey are given in reference table E, a brief summary of which is presented in table 33. The total universe for this survey consisted of 494,556 units.

As is usual for average informal sector units, particularly those in the rural areas, the income from the unit of the owning family was, on an average, less than even the imputed wage of

TABLE 33

Characteristics of informal sector industrial units, West Bengal, 1965-66

Item	Amount per unit
1. Average number of workers employed	2.25
of which (a) family labour	1.88
(b) hired labour	0.37
2. Value of assets (Rs)	1 421
3. Total value of production and work done for others (Rs)	4 043
4. Total cost of inputs (Rs)	2 454
of which (a) raw material	2 151
(b) fuel, electricity and lubricant	152
(c) work done through others	151
5. Total man-months worked	
(a) hired labour	3.50
(b) family labour	16.24
6. Depreciation (Rs)	117
7. Net value added by manufaeture [(3)—(4)—(6)] (Rs.)	1 472
of which (a) wage of hired labour, includiug casual labour	391
(b) imputed wage of family labour	1 814
(c) rent and interest	53
(d) profit for the entrepreneur	— 786

family labour. Taking total labour, both family and hired, net value added per man-month came to only Rs 74.57. This was an extremely low labour productivity but considering the levəl of income and, hence, of the level of living in India, the above income might not be considered inconsiderable, particularly if it was supplemented, as was often the case, by other income of the family.

Calcutta city claimed 31,115 such units or only 6.3 per cent of the total units in West Bengal. But in some of the specific industry groups, shares of Calcutta city were much higher as may be seen from table 34.

TABLE 34

Share of Calcutta city in the number of units in some selected informal sector industry groups, 1964/65

Industry group	Calcutta	West Bengal	Calcutta as % of West Bengal
(1)	(2)	(3)	(4)
1. Footwear, made up textile goods and leather products	6 767	44 220	15.3
2. Paper and printing	3 420	4 750	72.0
3. Rubber and chemical products	786	1 973	39.8
4. Metal products	3 406	30 712	11.1
5. Electrical machinery	1 456	2 594	56.1
6. Transport equipment	1 214	10 035	12.1
7. Jewellery	2 896	15 894	18.2
Total seven groups of industries	19 945	110 178	18.1

Area-wise separate reports for this survey have not yet been compiled. Some steps have been taken to compile detailed industry-wise reports. Only one such report on the food industry

TABLE 35

Percentage of units in the informal sector food industry having knowledge of the different facilities provided by different Government and semi-Government organisation, West Bengal, 1965/66

Types of facilities	% of units aware of the facility provided by the organisation							
	Directorate of Industries	Small Industries Service Institute	West Bengal Small Industries Corpn.	National Small Industries Corpn.	Board of Indus-tries	State Bank of India	West Bengal Financial Corpn.	Khadi and Cottage Industry Corpn.
(1)	(2)	(3)	(4)	(5)	(6)	(7)	(8)	(9)
1. On registration of units	0.54	—	—	—	—	—	—	0.62%
2. On technical know-how	0.28	—	—	—	—	—	—	—
3. On service centre facility	0.22	0.35	—	—	—	—	—	—
4. On marketing intelligence	0.22	—	0.42	0.14	—	—	—	—
5. On financial loan	2.48	—	—	—	1.02	2.31	0.79	
6. On hire purchase	—	—	0.13	0 18	—	—	—	—
7. On availability of raw material	—	—	0.15	—	—	—	—	—
8. On advice for preparing schemes		0.14	—	—	—	—	—	—
9. On facility of industrial estate	—	—	—	0.30	—	—	—	—

Source : Bureau of Economics and Statistics, Government of West Bengal.

has so far been published. The other industry reports including one for West Bengal as a whole have been compiled but not yet published. We wish to take up here all the published and so far unpublished reports because they do throw np some of the very important features of small, informal sector units which were never tackled earlier or hereafter in any other survey.

The most important of such findings revealed in the published report on the food industry relates to the role played by Government and its allied organisations in promoting industry and regarding the awareness of the units concerning the availability of such help.

It appears from the report that only 2,340 units or only 2.40 per cent of the total number of food-industry units in West Bengal numbering 97,504 could receive any "assistance" irrespective of the source of assistance. Out of these 2,340 units receiving assistance, only 3.03 per cent or 71 units received any assistance from Government and their allied agencies. These units represented 0.07 per cent of the total number of units in this industry. More startling, however, is the information on the knowledge of those units regarding the availability of such assistance from Government and government-sponsored organisations. Table 35 summarises the extent of knowledge these establishments possessed in this regard with respect to the various governmental organisations belonging to the State Government as well as to the Central Government.

Table 35 provides us with a glimpse of how removed these informal sector units were from any sort of promotional and development activity being undertaken, often with huge publicity and huge cost, by the Government and government-sponsored organisations belonging either to the States or to the Centre, often for the expressed purpose of helping these small units. The very first entry is crucial. Only 0.54 per cent of the units were aware that for obtaining any kind of government help it was necessary to have themselves registered with the Directorate of Industries—now the Directorate of Cottage and Small-Scale Industry. This percentage could be so low because almost none of them was aware that Government provided any facility at all. This is particularly painful not only because it meant that a relatively huge expenditure being incurred for setting up and for running those "developmental" organisations, specially meant for small industies, was most probably going to waste, but also because without a properly directed massive programme to provide initial help to all these units in inter-related fields (such as supply of inputs, credit, training, marketing, etc.) it would not be possible to make the small units break out of their socio-economic institutional limitations and stand on their own feet. Designing a mechanism of providing such a package of help will constitute the central focus for realising in full, inter alia, the employment and production potential of these informal sector units.

TABLE 36

Range of variation between the different broad industry groups with respect to some selected variables, informal sector industry, West Bengal, 1965/66

Items	Range of inter-industry variation		
	From	To	Ratio
(1)	(2)	(3)	(4)
1. Value of assets per unit (Rs.)	519	27 025	52.1
2. Hired labour per unit (number)	0.07	2.96	42.3
3. Family labour per unit (number)	1.23	2.45	2.0
4. Total cost of inputs per unit (Rs.)	466	15 845	34.0
5. Total depreciation per unit (Rs.)	11	732	66.5
6. Total value of output per unit (Rs.)	1 147	28 128	24.5
7. Total value added per unit (Rs.)	596	14 292	24.0
8. Total wage for hired labour per unit (Rs.)	85	5 828	68.6
9. Total imputed wage for family labour per unit (Rs.)	745	3 459	4.6
10. Total profit per unit (Rs)	- 2 465	4 719	–

We may now go back to the statistical presentation of the details for the different industry groups for West Bengal as a whole. The relevant data on these industries are presented in reference table F. It may be seen from this reference table that there is a wide variation between the 15 broad industry groups with respect to each of the variables under discussion. Thus, value of assets per unit varied from Rs 327 in the miscellaneous group of industries to Rs 27,025 in the industry group "structural clay products". The ranges of variation between the different industry groups for some of the more important variables are presented in table 36.

It may be be seen from table 36 that, leaving aside use of family labour, the range of variation with respect to each variable, presented above, was very wide. So far, as profit was concerned it was negative for ten groups and the highest loss was Rs 2,465 per unit; there was net profit in the remaining five groups with highest profit per unit reaching the level of Rs 4,719. The loss in the unit did not, however, signify that the owners did not earn any income from the unit. It only signified, as we have observed earlier, that the income they earned was less than what they should have obtained as wage payment if they could get a wage even at the rate at which they themselves paid their hired workers. And as family labour time was nearly five times that of hired labour in these informal sector units, the cheapness of the output of the informal sector results from an inhuman underpayment of wages or income to its work force. The low price of informal sector products matched well, on the one hand, with the demand for mainly cheap, low quality industrial goods from the poorer majority of consumers. It also added to the profits of large, organised units who could use the cheap labour to produce at low cost more sophisticated products (as also the cheap products) for sale under their own well known brand names at relatively very high prices. Thus, by keeping the poor satisfied with cheap consumption goods, and guaranteeing at the same time an excessive profit for big houses controlling the market, the small units today play an essential role in making the present economic structure function.

In contrast to the wide range of the variations presented

TABLE 37

Wage per man-month for the hired workers and net value added per man-month for all workers in the different informal sector industry groups, West Bengal, 1965/66

Industry group	Wage per man-month for hired workers	Total net value added per man-month of work (in Rupees)
(1)	(2)	(3)
1. Food	84	70
2. Beverage and tobacco	99	71
3. Textiles	94	29
4. Footwear, leather, etc.	125	200
5. Wood and cork excluding (6) below	121	96
6. Furniture and fixtures	155	84
7. Paper and printing	105	109
8. Rubber and chemicals	105	167
9. Structural clay products	244	376
10. Glass, etc.	161	45
11. Metal products and general machinery	130	127
12. Electrical machinery and appliances	113	124
13. Transport equipment	97	111
14. Jewellery, etc.	91	168
15. Miscellaneous	129	38
All industry	112	75

above, the variation in wages paid per man month to the hired worker was relatively far smaller, as shown in table 37. The table reveals that, while in the informal sector as a whole, value added per man-month of work done was lower than the average wage the units paid to their own hired workers, in seven out of the total 15 industry groups, the rate of value added was higher than the corresponding wage rate, although in two of these seven groups, rent and interest claimed such a high proportion that what remained as profit for the unit was actually lower than the imputed wage of family labour. Thus, only in five groups did the units earn income not only from the imputed wage of family labour but also from real net profit. In the remaining ten industry groups the income of the units was far less than even the imputed value of wage of family labour. This table clearly brings out that there was a wide gap between the different industry groups in respect of their average condition with respect to profit income.

The average for the various industry groups presented in reference table F and the overall average covering all the industry groups presented above in table 33 hide very wide fluctuation between the sub-groups within each group as well as between different industry groups. Thus, round the average net value added per unit of Rs 1,162 per year in the food industry as a whole, its range of intra-industry variation was as wide as Rs 118 to Rs 13,644. The ranges of variation between the different sub-groups within the same industry are presented in table 38 which shows very wide variations in all the variables under study and much wider variation between the sub-groups within each industry than between different industry groups. The variation in wages per man-month was relatively smaller.

Another interesting characteristic of the informal sector industrial entrepreneurs, more apparent in rural areas, was revealed in this 1965/66 survey. This aspect, however, was tabulated only for the Report on the Food Industry. In this industry group the average income of the families owning the industrial unit was Rs 2,096 per family per month (i.e. above poverty level); but of this average income, industry contributed only Rs 909 or 43 per cent of the total. Their other main source of income was agriculture. On an average each of these families owned nearly 1.88 acres (0.76 hectares) and, in addition, they leased-in

TABLE 38

Range of variation between the different sub-groups in each industry group with respect to some selected variables, informal sector industry, West Bengal, 1966

Industry group with no. of sub-groups	Range of variations in: Assets per unit (Rs.)	Hired labour per unit (No.)	Family labour per unit (No.)	Net value added per year per unit (Rs.)	Total value added by sub-groups (Rs. 000)
(1)	(2)	(3)	(4)	(5)	(6)
1. Food industry (14)	85—26 665	0—3.40	1.11—2.50	118—13 644	0.1— 40.9
2. Beverage and tobacco (2)	435— 1 866	1.08—1.19	1.44—1.91	1 776— 2 501	4.5— 51.0
3. Textile (11)	19— 5 426	0—2.53	1.61—2.98	95— 5 126	0.5— 54.2
4. Footwear, etc. (8)	183— 4 236	0.05—0.90	1.14—1.69	1 163— 3 808	0.7—134.6
5. Manuf. of wood and cork	202—19 276	0.01—1.97	1.41—1.92	306—10 406	0.4— 17.0
6. Manuf. of furniture and fixtures	2 532—10 245	0.10—2 08	1.19—1.80	1 119— 9 805	0.5— 13.4
7. Manuf. of paper products	3 267—19 182	0'66—3.56	1.22—1.53	1 828— 7 182	1.7— 9.5
8. Manuf. of rubber products	2 743—21 180	0 46—3.19	1.48—1.81	1 892—12 182	0.4— 5 2
9. Manuf. of struct. clay products	9 644—55 361	1.14—3 29	1.35—2.12	4 087—29 426	1.0— 44.5
10. Manuf. of glass and glass products	507— 4 444	0 03—2.05	1.25—2.38	681— 5 735	0.7— 28.7
11. Basic metal industry	515—16 013	0.11—4 45	1.29—1.88	631—14 944	0.6— 22.4
12. Manuf. of electrical machines	2 758— 7 438	0.70—2.19	1.30—1.53	2 669— 6 404	1.2— 10.2
13. Manuf. of transport equipment	437—11 132	0.17—3.15	1.33—1.73	1 152— 9 916	0.9— 27.1
14. Manuf. of jewellery	1 130— 1 319	0 17—0.21	1.33—1.52	1 211— 2 632	7.6— 19.5
15. Misc. manufacture	162—12 232	0,03—2.43	1.12—2.03	396— 8 788	0.6— 61.8
All sub-groups	19—26 665	0—3.56	1.11—2.98	95—29 426	0.1—134.6

an additional net 0.21 acres (0.08 hectares) making their operational holding equal to 2.09 acres (0.84 hectares) or little less than the average holding per agricultural family (including landless families) in rural West Bengal. This shows how closely rural industry was linked with the agricultural sector and how the income from informal sector industry supplemented the corresponding income from the agricultural and other sectors. Table 39 shows the percentage distribution of the total family income by the different sources.

TABLE 39

Percentage distribution of the total income of the families running small units by the source of their income, food industry, West Bengal, 1965/66

Item / Source of income	Total	Industry	Agriculture and allied	Trade	Others
(1)	(2)	(3)	(4)	(5)	(6)
Income per family per per year (Rs)	2 096	909	844	155	188
Percentage distribution	100.0	43.4	40.3	7.4	8.9

Like the other characteristics, the extent of dependence on industry as a source of income also varied widely between the different sub-groups. Thus, in this food industry, in certain sub-groups—non-power using rice pounding, bread and cake, and biscuits and other bakery—the share of industry in total family income was respectively as high as 88, 84 and 85 per cent. On the other hand, the corresponding share in other sub-groups —cane *gur* and palm *gur*—were as low as 5 and 13 per cent respectively.

Similarly, with regard to land ownership, variation was from 0.16 acres to 7.45 acres per family between the different sub-groups in food industry. With regard to leasing-in or leasing-out also, it was seen that while in average families in the 11 sub-groups of the food industry, there occurred a net leasing-out of land varying from 100 per cent of the owned land to only 2.3

per cent, in six sub-groups only there occurred net leasing-in and it varied from 86 per cent of the owned land to only 10 per cent.

The entire phenomenon of the pattern of linkages between agriculture and rural informal-sector industry needs to be analysed more thoroughly but this, however, is beyond the scope of this report, concerned as it is with the employment potential in informal-sector industry in the Calcutta area. Nevertheless, the above discussion about the agriculture-industry integration should not be considered a digression because—as may become apparent later—the realisation of the full employment potential of the metropolitan informal-sector industry is vitally linked up with modernised agriculture, one of whose many facets will be integration of agriculture and industry in the rural areas.

3.6. Survey of the non-registered manufacturing sector urban West Bengal 1970/71

In 1970/71, the Bureau of Applied Economics and Statistics, Government of West Bengal, conducted two simultaneous surveys on unorganised manufacturing. One of these two covered all the industrial units employing one to four persons, on a sample basis, situated in urban areas of West Bengal. The other one covered all the remaining units in the unorganised informal sector, viz., the units employing five to nine persons if using power or five to nineteen persons if not using power. This latter survey was also confined to the urban areas of West Bengal. Provisional, and as yet unpublished, data thrown up by these two surveys will be summarised in this section.

The relevant data pertaining to the first survey are presented in table 40. The table reveals that in 1971 these very small units employed 116,000 persons in Calcutta city proper, and they constituted nearly 32 per cent of all such units in urban West Bengal as a whole. The corresponding share of these Calcutta city units in the total income generated was 39 per cent. The disproportionate domination of the city of Calcutta in this sphere may be clear from the above data.

One of the main characteristics of these very small units in the informal sector is the domination of family labour in the

TABLE 40

Characteristics of small industrial units employing one to four workers in the different urban areas of West Bengal, 1971 (Value in Rs. millions ; employment in '000)

Items	(1) Calcutta	(2) Howrah	(3) Other urban areas of West Bengal	(4) Total urban area of West Bengal	(5) Percentage share of Calcutta (1)÷(4)
1. No. of units	46 930	11 382	99 199	157 511	31.5
2. Total productive capital	107	60	172	338	31.6
3. Total employment	116	31	228	375	30 9
(a) Family workers	68	18	168	254	26.8
(b) Hired workers	48	13	60	121	39.7
4. Total value of raw material	234	144	381	759	30.8
5. Total value of output sold	338	177	512	1 027	32.9
6. Gross value added of which :	104	33	131	268	38.8
(a) Wages to hired employees	66	15	60	141	46 8
(b) Imputed wage for family labour	93	21	182	296	31.4
(c) Gross surplus for the owners	—55	—3	—111	—169	32.5
(d) Net income for working proprietors	38	18	71	127	29.9

working force. Of the estimated total employment of 116,000 in these units in the Calcutta city area, 68,000 or nearly 59 per cent were family workers. The corresponding figures for urban West Bengal as a whole were 375,000 and 254,000. Thus in urban West Bengal, excluding Calcutta city, 186,000 workers out of a total of 259,000 or nearly 71 per cent of the total, were family workers.

The most important characteristic of this employment of family labour is that their earnings from the unit as worker-proprietors were less than what would have been their income from an imputed wage at the rate they themselves pay their hired workers. Thus, in Calcutta city, while the average wage per hired worker per year was Rs 1,375, the average annual income per family worker (including imputed wage) per year was as low as Rs 559, i.e. far less than even half of what they paid to their hired workers. The number of family workers per average establishment being 1.59 ; the total family income from working and running the enterprise was Rs 889 per year.

The poverty line, as defined in India now, is an income of about Rs 460 per capita per year at 1971 prices, or Rs 2,300 per family of five persons per year. It may be remembered in this connection that the Nutrition Committee, appointed by the Planning Commission, Government of India, recommended a figure of Rs 40 per capita per month at 1961 prices for defining the poverty level. Despite this recommendation which, incidentally, would have put almost the whole of India's population below the poverty line, the officially accepted poverty line was defined, without stating any rationale thereof, at Rs 20 per capita per month or Rs 240 per capita per year at 1961 prices. Due to the intervening price rise, the latter has increased to about Rs 460 per capita per year in 1971.

It may, thus, be seen that average income of the working proprietor families was less than 40 per cent of what was even officially defined as the poverty line. So far as the hired workers were concerned, assuming that there are 1.5 workers per family with five members at the same wage level, their total family income may be estimated at Rs 2,062, i.e. less than the poverty line though, obviously, not to the same extent as their employers.

A further point to be remembered in this connection is that in the previous table "gross value added" has been calculated by deducting only the value of raw materials from the value of output. The cost of depreciation, fuel, if any, used, etc., has not been taken into consideration because those data were not readily available. As the incomes of the working proprietors were deduced by subtracting only the wage of hired workers from the above gross value added, it is clear that the actual income of the working proprietors was even less than what has been stated above.

The conditions for all other areas were worse, with the possible exception of Howrah. These data have been summarised on the basis of the assumption made above, as shown in table 41. The poverty levels of both the wage workers and particularly of working proprietors, are apparent from the table and it becomes more apparent from a visit to the areas—mostly slums—with a concentration of such units. What, however, would not become apparent either from the table or from just a visit to these areas, is that in many cases these extremely low levels of earnings are

TABLE 41

Estimated income per family of hired workers and of working proprietors from the small industrial units employing less than five workers in the different urban areas of West Bengal, 1971

(in Rs.)

Earning per year per family	Calcutta	Howrah	Other urban areas	Total urban West Bengal
1. Hired workers (Rs.)*	2 062	1 731	1 500	1 748
2. Working proprietors (Rs.)	810	1 581	716	806
3. No. of family workers per unit	1.45	1.58	1.69	1.61

* It is assumed that there are 1.5 workers per family of five members in the hired workers' families, earning the same wage.

not a consequence of their technological inefficiency leading to production of inferior goods. With an in-depth study of these units, it becomes clear that many of these small units are the actual producers, manufacturers of goods which are ultimately marketed under well known, often internationally-famous, brand names ; in the public image, as well as officially, the latter appear as the manufacturing units but in practice they are partly, and often basically, nothing but trading units making large profits through marketing of goods actually produced by those anonymous "inefficient", backward poverty-stricken producers. We shall deal with this point in somewhat greater detail later.

Income or labour productivity is measured with reference to ex-factory price which may differ from the price paid by actual customers. For actually producing organised large units, the difference between ex-factory price and the price the ultimate

TABLE 42

Gross value added per worker, per unit of productive capital employment, and as a percentage of value of output, in the small units employing less than five workers, 1971
(Rs.)

Characteristic	Calcutta	Howrah	Other urban areas	Total urban West Bengal
1. Gross value added per worker	897	1 064	575	715
2. Productive capital per worker	922	2 000	754	901
3. Gross value added per rupee of productive capital employed	0.97	0.55	0.76	0.79
4. Gross value added per establishment	2 217	2 899	1 321	1 701
5. Gross value added as percentage of total output	30.8%	18.6%	25.6%	26.0%

consumer pays may not be very wide. In this context comparison of labour productivity or the capital-output ratio between the large and very small units may have an economic significance—because these will demonstrate the actual money income received in those enterprises—but it may not have much significance from the technological, physical productivity point of view.

The above observations need to be remembered while comparing ratios presented earlier in this report, and also those presented in table 42. Very low gross value added per worker (including family workers), and also per establishment, may be noted and appraised in the background of what has been stated above. Also to be noted is the extremely low value for productive capital required to employ one worker as well as that required to produce a unit of value added. The higher level of productivity as well as the higher level of investment for Howrah are due to the larger share of engineering units in the industry mix at Howrah compared to other areas.

We may now take up the next group of informal-sector units employing five to nine workers, if using power, or five to nineteen workers, if not using power. The relevant broad data for this group as a whole are presented in table 43. It may be seen from the table that although Calcutta city claimed only 38 per cent at the total units in the informal sector (excluding the units employing one to four workers), its corresponding share of such power-using units was as high as 52 per cent. Again, Calcutta units claimed 51 per cent of total fixed capital investment, 50 per cent of total working capital, 43 per cent of total output, and 46 per cent of total value added produced in those informal sector units in urban West Bengal as a whole. In reference tables G and H the relevant data, separately for each of the 20 major industry groups, have been presented respectively for Calcutta city and urban Howrah. A summary of these two reference tables with respect to the five most important industry group in these two areas, from the point of view of total net value added, is presented in table 44.

These five industry groups claimed 48 per cent of employment and 51 per cent of value added in their corresponding totals for Calcutta city. The corresponding shares in urban

TABLE 43

Characteristics of small industrial units employing 5 to 19 persons if not using power and 5 to 9 persons if using power, Calcutta and urban West Bengal, 1971
(Employment in '000 ; and value in Rs. million)

Items	Calcutta	Rest of urban West Bengal	Total urban West Bengal
1. Number of units :			
(a) Total	2 908	4 705	7 613
(b) With power	1 244	1 142	2 386
2. Total employment	23	38	61
3. Total productive capital	66	63	129
(a) Fixed capital	38	36	74
(b) Working capital	28	27	55
4. Total input	171	241	412
5. Depreciation	3	3	6
6. Total output	236	319	555
7. Net value added	63	74	137
(a) Wages and salaries	26	31	57
(b) Surplus	37	43	80

Howrah were higher ; respectively 51 per cent and 73 per cent, owing to the far greater weight of the engineering industry in Howrah. In Calcutta, the share of all engineering industry groups in the net value added of the totality of all industry groups in this section of the informal sector was only 27 per cent ; it was 66 per cent in Howrah. In absolute volume, however, even the informal sector engineering industry in Calcutta city was substantially bigger than that of Howrah. Thus, while the informal sector engineering units at Calcutta generated more than Rs. 14 million value added in 1970/71, the corresponding volume of Howra hwas below Rs. 14 million. Moreover, the industrial structure in Calcutta city was far more diversified than that for Howrah. Thus, in Calcutta, out of 20 industry groups, in seven there were more than 200 units each, and in 10 there were more than 100 units each. In Howrah, there were

TABLE 44

Characteristics of five important informal sector industry groups in Calcutta and urban Howrah, 1970/71 (units employing 5-9 persons, if using power, and 5-19 if not using power)

Items	Textiles (23)		Metal products (35)		Printing and allied (28)		Food industry (20)		General machinery (36)	
	Calcutta	Howrah	Calcutta	Howrah	Calcutta	Howrah	Calcutta	Howrah	Calcutta	Howrah
(1)	(2)	(3)	(4)	(5)	(6)	(7)	(8)	(9)	(10)	(11)
1. Total number of units	367	83	331	350	391	11	221	56	93	146
2. Total employment (including family workers)	2 818	758	2 493	2 549	2 953	87	2 019	474	680	1 060
3. Total net productive capital (Rs. '000) of which :	11 728	1 143	7 484	7 955	10 095	304	5 454	1 171	3 096	4 527
(a) owned fixed	4 944	382	1 904	1 824	5 139	120	1 104	197	1 081	1 894
(b) rented fixed	1 091	256	1 913	2 788	2 920	69	1 764	431	956	1 040
(c) working capital	5 693	505	3 667	3 343	2 036	115	2 586	543	1 059	1 593

(Contd.)

TABLE 44 (Contd.)

Characteristics of five important informal sector industry groups in Calcutta and urban Howrah, 1970/71
(units employing 5—9 persons, if using power, and 5–19 if not using power)

Items	Textiles (23)		Metal products (35)		Printing and allied (28)		Food industry (20)		General machinery (36)	
	Calcutta	Howrah	Calcutta	Howrah	Calcutta	Howrah	Calcutta	Howrah	Calcutta	Howrah
(1)	(2)	(3)	(4)	(5)	(6)	(7)	(8)	(9)	(10)	(11)
4. Total value of output (Rs. '000)	48 984	6 455	28 250	35 680	13 990	971	46 051	13 861	6 299	10 956
5. Total value of input (Rs. '000)	39 383	5 128	20 795	27 217	188	733	39 235	11 606	3 837	7 256
of which :										
(a) raw materials	38 161	5 043	19 840	25 298	175	715	37 553	11 139	3 510	6 772
(b) other	1 222	85	995	1 919	13	18	1 682	467	327	484
6. Depreciation (Rs '000)	380	43	274	329	633	16	220	59	145	224
7. Net value added (Rs. '000) (4-5-6)	9 221	1 284	7 181	8 134	6 638	222	6 596	2 196	2 317	3 476
8. Total paid-out wages (Rs. '000)	3 141	610	2 717	2 676	3 535	85	2 194	480	820	1 132
9. Total income of the proprietor workers (Rs. '000)	6 080	674	4 464	5 458	3 100	137	4 402	1 716	1 497	2 344

TABLE 45

Ratios relating to capital, labour and value added for five important informal sector industry groups, Calcutta and urban Howarh, 1970/71

(in Rs.)

Item	Area	Textiles	Metal Products	Printing and allied	Food	General machinery	All industyy groups
(1)	(2)	(3)	(4)	(5)	(6)	(7)	(8)
1. Productive capital per worker	Calcutta	4 162	3 002	3 419	2 701	4 553	2 865
	Howrah	1 508	3 121	3 494	2 470	4 271	2 802
2. Value added per worker	Calcutta	3 272	2 880	2 248	3 267	3 407	2 731
	Howrah	1 694	3 191	2 552	4 633	3 279	2 752
3. Value added per unit of productive capital	Calcutta	0.786	0.959	0.657	1.210	0.748	0.953
	Howrah	1.123	1.022	0.730	1.876	0.768	0.982

only two industry groups with more than 100 units in each, and both of these belonged to the engineering industry groups.

A comparison between these two areas with regard to capital per worker, value added per worker and value added per unit productive capital for the above five industry groups reveals interesting results. The relevant data are presented in table 45 which shows that in all the five industry groups as well as for all the 20 industry groups taken together the Howrah area used less, and often substantially less, to produce unit income. The ratios for Howrah are also in general more favourable than for the Calcutta area.

3.7. CONDITION OF FAMILIES

In 1974, the Labour Department, Government of West Bengal, conducted a pilot study regarding the total income and expenditure of the families of workers engaged in informal sector industries in Calcutta city. This was a small study covering only 123 workers in ten industry and trade groups. The relevant information obtained from the survey is given in table 46.

The average size of these 123 families was 4.38 and they had, on an average, 0.28 earners, in addition to the sampled worker working in the informal sector. Thus, on an average, the earner/dependent ratio in these families was 0.29, and these families depended mainly on the earning of the worker in the informal sector. Average income of these families come to Rs 3,052 per year or Rs 58 per capita per month. The income was no doubt low, but it was above what has officially been defined as the poverty line. Thus these families belonged, from the point of view of level of earning or of expenditure, to the upper 30 per cent of the West Bengal population, because it was estimated that even in 1972 70 per cent of the West Bengal population was below the poverty line. What this income for these fortunate families belonging to the upper 30 per cent of the population could provide them may be clear from the pattern of their expenditure, and more concretely from the level of caloric intake assured by that expenditure pattern. The relevant data are presented in table 47.

From table 46 it was clear that the total consumption expen-

TABLE 46

Condition of the families which supplied workers to the informal sector industry and trade, Calcutta city, 1974
(Values in Rs.)

Industry	No. of sample workers	Size of the family	Average no. of other earners in the family	Average weekly income per family from all sources	Average weekly expenditure per family				
					Food	Clothing	Housing	Others	Total
1. Tailoring	8	5.38	0.25	60.60	39.94	4.91	4.10	13.80	62.75
2. Printing	66	4.61	0.30	67.05	45.10	3.47	5 07	15.32	68.96
3. Powerloom	4	5.00	0.50	56.52	38.12	3.51	4.27	13.31	59.21
4. Hosiery	8	3.75	0.25	53.52	35.72	2.87	7.12	11.43	57.14
5. Hotels and restaurants	5	2.40	0.20	29.40	19.47	1.32	3.76	7.80	32.35
6. Shops	7	3.71	0.14	47.13	30.15	2.26	6.56	11.46	50.43
7. Nursing homes	4	2.50	0.25	44.94	28 48	3 69	6.37	8.73	47.27
8. Tannery	7	3.00	—	41.70	28.26	2 25	5.07	11.56	47.14
9. Bone mills	6	4.25	0.50	53.54	37.50	1.53	4.50	11.39	54.92
10. Rubber	8	4.75	0.38	64.40	38.28	2.73	9.72	15 36	66.09
Total	123	4.38	0 28	58.70	*	*	*	*	*

TABLE 47

Per capita consumption pattern on different food items, and the resultant total calorie consumption in the families supported by workers of unorganised industries situated within the jurisdiction of the Calcutta Corporation

Food items	Tailoring	Printing	Powerloom	Hosiery	Hotels and Rest's	Shops	Nursing homes	Tannery	Bone Mills	Rubber
Food consumption pattern per adult per day (in kg.) :										
Rice	0.170	0.142	0.205	0.186	0.162	0.163	0.191	0.194	0.205	0.197
Wheat	0.153	0.157	0 124	0.129	0.118	0.134	0.117	0.154	0.153	0.114
Dal	0.031	0.040	0.047	0.035	0.029	0.038	0.043	0.053	0.050	0.024
Total cereals	0.354	0.339	0.376	0.350	0.309	0.335	0.351	0.401	0.408	0.335
Mustard oil	0.015	0.029	0.019	0.017	0.014	0.015	0.017	0.015	0.012	0.079
Sugar/gur	0.043	0 032	0.041	0 045	0.022	0 032	0 042	0.042	0 045	0.015
Potato	0.050	0.044	0.061	0.056	0.031	0.053	0 047	0 067	0.053	0.027
Onion	0.023	0 037	0 033	0.028	0 025	0.027	0.031	0.019	0.015	0 017
Fish	0 026	0.049	0.032	0.029	0.021	0.025	0.044	0.026	0 019	0.050
Calorie consumption per adult per day (calorie units)	1 586	1 682	1 707	1 608	1 326	1 478	1 620	1 765	1 754	1 576

diture of the families in the sample was slightly higher than total income, denoting a marginal net dis-saving. In spite of this dis-saving, however, their expenditure put them above the officially defined poverty line ; but it could provide them with an average calorie consumption of only 1,650 per day – while the minimum required for an ordinary adult is considered to be about 2,500. It is better not to raise the question of the protein needed to supplement the calories.

CHAPTER IV

SURVEY OF SLUM INDUSTRIES IN THE CALCUTTA AREA

4.1. INTRODUCTION

The survey of slum industries in the Calcutta area discussed in this chapter was undertaken in the first three months of 1974. It was specifically designed for the purpose of the present study, which was initially conceived, as stated in Chapter 1, as an investigation to find out the employment potential in the slum industry in the Calcutta area and the mechanism for realising this potential in practice. In course of preparing for the survey in designing and pre-testing the schedule, and in course of training the investigators (see Annex A), it gradually became clear to us that it was necessary to widen the canvas of the study even to fulfil the original limited purpose of the survey. However, in the survey schedule as such, this new consciousness could not be fully reflected. Nevertheless, the survey was very useful because it not only vitally supplemented the available information from other surveys, summarised in the previous chapter, but it also provided an opportunity to re-establish direct, personal contacts between the staff of the State Planning Board, Government of West Bengal, and the small units in metropolitan Calcutta. Such direct contacts with the highest policy recommending authorities are an essential pre-requisite not only for suggesting realistic and correct policies, but also for its relatively speedier and efficient implementation, once the policy is accepted by the Government.

One of the vital aspects of the survey was concerned with finding out the specific difficulties faced by these units with regard to government help, credit, marketing, etc. But the relevant data on these points could not be gathered in a satisfactory way, and these were not even tabulated for the purpose of analysing the results of the survey.

Our inability to obtain these vital pieces of information itself was a very important finding. It provided us with an insight as to the precondition for obtaining such information on a mass scale, as is normally expected in a census or a large sample survey. In a society where the poorer majority have to depend even for their very minimum livelihood, or for means to obtain that livelihood, on the richer few, it is not possible for the poor man to speak out in an explicit fashion to an investigator on the harsh, inequitable, unjust treatment he receives from the rich and from the powerful. A small unit supplying goods to a large industrial unit or to the trader or to the *dadandar* (a man who advances money or/and raw material against future delivery of produce, often at less than half the market price), cannot possibly speak out against the person concerned under normal circumstances. This inability arises from the fact that if that powerful man concerned refuses to purchase the small unit's goods even at that reduced price, the poor man will have no alternative but to keep his goods unsold and be completely ruined. So long as the choice is between thus getting ruined immediately, or leading a life subservient to the richer few controlling the market and the capital, hoping to survive at least for some time, most of the poor cannot but inevitably choose the latter alternative. This choice, however, does not save him permanently. As we have noticed in the previous chapter (sec. 3.4.), more than 12 per cent of the units had to succumb before the economic forces now operating which condemn the small units to purchase at a relatively higher price and sell at a relatively lower price. Only with the emergence of a third possibility, the possibility of freeing themselves from the need for the "mercy" of the rich, when there will be a provision of easy and timely credit at a rate at which larger units now get it, a guarantee of supplying an adequate quantity of appropriate inputs at a price at the proper time, just as the large units now manage to get them, and a guarantee of providing efficient outlets to market their finished goods at a price at which the large units now sell them in the ultimate market, may we expect an average poor producer—and almost all the slum producers are poor—to speak out openly regarding the causes behind the real difficulties they face.

Most of these difficulties arise from the existing socio-economic structure itself. Despite this, there are many difficulties arising from the pattern of functioning of present socio-economic institutions rather than from their existence as such. It is not only possible and necessary to modify the pattern in favour of the poor producers, it is mainly through such an attempt that the small producers can get themselves organised for contributing effectively to the vitally necessary process of basically changing the present socio-economic structure. Thus, for example it may not be possible to remove the difficulties that arise from the very existence and functioning of very powerful oligopolistic, mainly commercial, houses without changing the basic socio-economic structure, but it should certainly be possible to make the poorer producers aware of, and then take advantage of, the numerous good facilities which have already been created by the Government at a huge cost specifically for benefiting the poor. It is only through such an attempt that the poor producers may not only start to improve their lot to some extent, but may also begin to have a conviction that something much bigger can perhaps be achieved.

Without such a conviction, it will not be possible for the small units to get themselves organised to achieve what is due to them, and to perform efficiently the role allotted to the informal sector by history in this part of the world, viz. to provide a viable livelihood to the majority of the people.

The above observation has been further confirmed from the rural areas by the work now being done in implementing the Comprehensive Area Development Programme (CADP). It has been our experience that no plan for really benefiting the masses of the people can be prepared without an active involvement of the people concerned ; and the people, particularly from the lower strata, can participate in the planning process once they can feel that something really is going to be done. The best way to make them feel this was to start really doing something so that the credibility gap could be removed to some extent. The key tasks for enabling the informal sector, in its major wing in the rural areas in the field of agriculture and cottage industry, as well as in its minor wing in the urban areas centred round small industry and trade, to perform its historic role are to utilise the facilities provided by the existing situation and to effect a basic change in the present situation, to provide a strong technical administrative organisation initially from outside and to develop the people's own co-operative organisations eventually to run their own affairs within one to three years, and to provide an optimum initial subsidy and then to make the people ultimately fully self-reliant and "credit-worthy".

Reverting back to our slum-industry survey, it may be stated that despite our inability to generate adequate statistical, quantitative information from the survey, the survey equipped us : (a) by providing vital qualitative information and understanding through some type studies in depth of some of the units and this understanding includes what can be said to be the prerequisite for quantifying that qualitative information ; (b) by providing the State Planning Organisation of the Government of West Bengal with a very living contact with the urban informal sector, the contacts which are continuing long after the completion of the formal survey. This living personal contact may fulfil one of the preconditions mentioned above, viz., integrating planning with implementation for the mutual benefit of both. This is already being crystallised in what may be called a Comprehensive Area Development Programme for urban areas, and by its very nature, the urban CADP, just like the rural CADP to which it will be complementary, will have to base itself on the small man working in the informal sector. Some of the initial stages of the crystallisation of this thinking may become apparent in a later chapter dealing with the programme for development of the West Bengal economy as a whole.

The development of urban CADPs will create the basis, as is already happening in the case of rural CADPs, for small people themselves to come forward not only with their problems but also with an implementation plan for solving them. In this endeavour, this survey and the admirable band of social workers from the Calcutta Urban Service Consortium (CUSCON), the CMPO and the CMDA who carried it out will have played very useful roles.

4.2 The Findings of the Survey

For the purpose of conducting the survey, slum areas with marked concentration of informal sector units were chosen and then grouped into the 11 zones shown in table 48. The original number of units selected was 640.

Table 48

Distribution of the sampled units by their location in different survey zones, survey of slum industries, Calcutta area, 1974

Serial No.	Name of survey zones	No. of industrial units
1.	Howrah city North	20
2.	Howrah city Central	210
3.	Howrah city South	101
4.	Cossipore, Baranagar, Paikpara, Datta Bagan (northern suburb of Calcutta)	139
5.	Kidderpore, Matiaburuz, Santoshpore (South-West Calcutta)	70
6.	Chetla (South-Central Calcutta)	19
7.	Baithak Khana, Rajabagan, Narikel-danga, Fulbagan (Central Calcutta)	20
8.	Beliaghata, Manicktola, Bagmari (North-East Calcutta)	19
9.	Entally-Park Circus (Central East Calcutta)	7
10.	Jorabagan, Rambagan, Kumartolly, Chorbagan (North-West Calcutta)	26
11.	Tangra-Tiljala (East Calcutta)	9
Total :	All survey zones.	640

The survey zones were thus dispersed throughout Calcutta and Howrah cities and the immediate suburbs. During the course of the actual survey, nine more units were added to make the sample size 649. These 649 units covered 56 types of industries

TABLE 49

Distribution of units and their employment by industry group and employment size classes, selected Calcutta area slums, 1974

Industry group	Number of units and their total employment in the size class									
	1—4 employees		5—9 employees		10—19 employees		20+ employees		Total	
	Empl.	Units	Empl.	Units	Empl.	Units	Empl.	Units	Empl.	Units
(1)	(2)	(3)	(4)	(5)	(6)	(7)	(8)	(9)	(10)	(11)
1. Food and tobacco	77	27	164	25	42	3	—	—	283	55
2. Textiles	64	23	107	16	174	13	95	2	340	54
3. Wood	129	49	80	14	22	2	69	2	300	67
4. Paper	12	4	38	6	—	—	—	—	50	10
5. Printing	19	8	33	5	14	1	—	—	66	14
6. Leather	30	10	73	12	43	3	47	2	193	27
7. Rubber	6	3	20	3	10	1	—	—	36	8
8. Chemicals	81	27	264	37	262	21	41	2	648	87
9. Non-metallic mineral products	29	8	95	15	128	11	221	4	473	38
10. Metal products (excluding machinery)	170	57	565	85	282	23	168	5	1 185	170
11. Machinery	87	29	229	34	171	12	71	2	558	77
12. Miscellaneous	59	22	96	14	46	3	—	—	201	39
Total	766	267	1 774	266	1 194	93	712	19	4 443	646

Note : There is a discrepancy of 3 units.

which were then grouped under 12 broad industry groups. The survey results in the following paragraph will be presented in terms of the 12 industry groups.

The 649 units together employed 4,446 persons. The distribution of these units along with their employment by 12 industry groups and for the four following employment size classes has been presented in table 49 :

size class 1—units employing 1-4 persons
2—units employing 5-9 persons
3—units employing 10-19 persons
4—units employing 20 or more persons.

It may be seen from the table that by far the most important industry group in the Calcutta area slums is the engineering industry which includes industry groups 10 (metal products) and 11 (machinery) in the table. These two groups together claimed more than 40 per cent of the total number of units and nearly the same propotion of employment in the units covered by this survey. As expected, most of the units in the slum areas were small and nearly 80 per cent of the units had less than ten persons per unit in those factories. But there were also quite a few (19) relatively large units employing on an average about 40 persons.

It is interesting to find out that even in the Calcutta area, more than 60 per cent of the units were not registered, either as a factory under the Factory Act (owing to the fact that they did not fall within the scope of the Act), or with the Directorate of Cottage and Small-Scale Industries. The latter registration is voluntary but only such a registration can enable them to receive any sort of government help. Out of 649 units only 180, or less than 28 per cent, were registered with the Directorate of Cottage and Small-Scale Industries as a small-scale unit. The summary information on this point for industrial units taken together is given in table 50.

This relatively meagre coverage of registration shows either that most of the units even in the Calcutta area are not aware of the various facilities that the Government may be offering, or even if they are aware of the facilities, they do not

TABLE 50

Distribution of the industrial units in the informal sector in selected Calcutta area slums, by the extent of registration with relevant government organisation, 1974

Item	Total employment	No. of units	% of units
1. Registration only as small-scale industries unit with Director of SSI	1 601	164	25.2
2. Registered only under Factory Act	189	20	3.1
3. Registered both as small scale and under Factories Act	253	16	2.5
4. Not registered	2 393	449	69.2
Total	4 438[a]	649	100.0

a There is discrepancy of eight persons in total employment figure.

think that such facilities can actually be made available to them, or it is too troublesome to get themselves registered ; and hence their apathy in getting themselves registered. The other side of the picture is the lack of extension work even in Calcutta city by the relevant government departments for convincing the units that it may be possible to improve their functioning by getting government help.

A very important aspect of this informal sector industry group may become apparent if we refer to the type of space the industries use for the manufacturing purposes. Leaving aside the four units for which data are not available, of the remaining 645 units, only 241 or 37 per cent of the total units operate in spaces exclusively set apart for industry. The remaining 63 per cent of the units operate either from a space which is used mainly for residence or used for both residence and industry. The relevant data in this connection are given in table 51. It may be seen that the industrial units operating from spaces meant for industry alone are only marginally bigger sized units with an average employment of nearly eight per unit, compared to the remaining units with an average employment of about six persons.

TABLE 51

Extent of joint use of space of the different industrial units in the Calcutta area, 1974

Item	Employment	Unit	% of units
1. Space mainly for residence	1 042	160	24.8
2. Both for industry and residence	1 353	229	35.5
3. Mainly for industry	100	15	2.3
4. For industry only	1 918	241	37.4
Total	4 413	645	100.0

(Relevant data for four units employing 33 persons not available)

So far as the nature of construction of the sheds and buildings now being used by these informal sector units is concerned, it appears that as many as 72 per cent of the units work in a space in which only the roof is *kucha* i.e. the floor and the walls are of bricks and cement. The remaining units are more

TABLE 52

Distribution of the units by the availability of covered space per unit in the Calcutta area slum industries, 1974[a]

Total covered space per unit (in sq. ft.)	No. of units	Total employment	Per cent Units	Per cent employment
1. Below 100	120	497	19	11.4
2. 100-249	184	1 028	29	23.6
3. 250-499	141	870	22	19.9
4. 500 and above	193	1 966	30	45.1
Total	638	4 361	100	100.0

a Relevant data for 11 units employing 82 persons could not be gathered.

or less evenly balanced, 15 per cent using all *kucha* sheds while the remaining 13 per cent use all *pucca* space.

The congested conditions in which these small units operate may be seen from the fact that nearly 48 per cent of the units work with space below 250 sq. ft. per unit and only 30 per cent of the units had 500 sq. ft. and above per unit. As expected, the units with less space are relatively smaller sized units while those with larger space per unit are relatively larger units. The relevant data are summarised in table 52.

TABLE 53

Distribution of the units by the number of days they worked during the year 1973

No. of days worked	No. of units	Total employment	Percentage of units
(1)	(2)	(3)	(4)
1. Below 100 days	27	150	4.3
2. 100 to 199 days	82	438	12.9
3. 200 to 249 days	80	590	12.6
4. 250 to 299 days	112	844	17.7
5. 300 days and above	333	2.353	52.5
Total	634	4 372	100.0

Table 54 deals with one of the most significant manifestations of underutilisation of capacity in small industries, the relative absence of multiple shift operation. What is in a way most striking in the table is that there is not much difference in the extent of multiple shift operation in the smaller three of the four size classes within the informal sector. While in the smallest two-size classes only 4.4 per cent and 4.6 per cent of the total employment in those size classes were in the units working multiple shifts, in the next higher class, employing 10 to 19 workers, the proportion is only marginally higher : 6.6 per cent.

TABLE 54

Distribution of units and employment by the number of shifts they work in the different employment size classes, Calcutta slum area units, 1974

Item	1—4 persons		5—9 persons		10—19 persons		20 and more persons		Total	
	Unit	Empl.	Unit	Empl.	Unit	Empl.	Unit	Empl.	Unit	Empl.
(1)	(2)	(3)	(4)	(5)	(6)	(7)	(8)	(9)	(10)	(11)
Units working in one shift only	256	741	255	1 687	88	1 120	15	446	614	3 994
Units working in two shifts per day	10	30	11	77	4	59	2	85	27	251
Units working in three shifts per day	1	2	X	X	1	15	2	181	4	198
Total	267	773	266	1764	92	1 194	19	712	645	4 443
% of units and their employment in multiple shift operation	4.1	4.4	4.1	4.62	5.4	6.6	21.1	59.6	4 8	11.2

Note : There is a discrepancy of four units.

But in the size class having units with 20 and more workers, the corresponding proportion is as high as 59.6 per cent. In this size class also, the multiple shift units are the bigger ones with average employment of more than 66 persons.

It may be seen from table 55 that 95 per cent of the small units in the Calcutta slum area operate in single shift and they together account for 89 per cent of total employment. Even if we leave aside the very small units employing less than five workers, and if the remaining single shift units could operate just two shifts, then employment would increase by 3,253 persons, an increase by 73 per cent of the total employment in all the units in the sample. However, apart from the basic constraints for achieving fuller capacity utilisation in the inadequate supply of input and credit at the organised market price, there are other difficulties for these units for operating in multiple shifts. One is their direct linkage with residence : production space of 60 per cent of the units is also used for residence. Another is that family based management makes it difficult to provide supervision and management in a second shift ; moreover, when there is sufficient work, the single shift often extends far beyond the normal 8 hours per day.

Next we may take up the distribution of units by the amount of machinery, in money terms, used by the different units. It may be seen from the data in table 55 that 43 per cent of the units used less than only Rs 1,500 per unit for machinery and only 23 per cent of the units used more than Rs 10,000 per unit for the machinery. It should, therefore, be clear that there is a considerable amount of machinery even in the slum units and their productivity can certainly be dramatically increased if the various institutional constraints to which they are subjected can be removed. Total value of machinery of these 609 units came to Rs 6,149,000, of which only Rs 135,000 was foreign. Thus, these units had, on an average, Rs 10,000 worth of machinery per unit each with an employment, on an average, of 6·87 persons. This means that these units used only Rs 1,470 worth of machinery per worker of which, on an average, foreign machinery constituted as little as Rs 32 per person.

The extremely low value, compared to that in the organised

TABLE 55

Distribution of industrial units by the amount of machinery used by them in Calcutta area slum industries, 1974

Amount of machinery used by the unit (in Rs.)	No. of units	Total employment	Percentage distribution of units
(1)	(2)	(3)	(4)
1. Below Rs 500	143	676	23.5
2. Rs 500—1,499	117	612	19.2
3. Rs 1,500—2,999	89	586	14.6
4. Rs 3,000—9,999	121	808	19.9
5. Rs 10,000—24,999	86	773	14.1
6. 25,000 and above	53	727	8.7
	609	4 182	100.0

sector, of both the actual, as well as the potential, value of machinery required to employ one person in the slum industries and also the very low proportion of foreign machinery in these units, should be noted. Against the background of capital scarcity and particularly of foreign exchange, and growing unemployment, the technology pursued in these units appears to have a very important significance for the totality of the economy.

The total amount of working capital used by the totality of 649 units came to Rs. 9,219,000, i.e. Rs 14,200 per unit, which came to only Rs 2,075 per employed person.

Estimated value of owned land and buildings, which evidently includes the entire space used wholly or partly for industrial purposes, came to Rs 2,323,000. Corresponding monthly rent for the rented space came to Rs 44,000. Estimating the value of land and buildings of rented buildings as equivalent to ten years' purchase, it came to Rs 5,280,000 for those rented buildings, making a total of Rs 7,603,000 for land and buildings. Assuming that 50 per cent of that space, on an average, was used for industry, per unit fixed capital for land and buildings came to about Rs 5,900 per unit or Rs 855 per person.

The data above on capital use are summarised in table 57. The relevancy of the particular production technology pursued

TABLE 56

Capital use per establishment and per worker in the Calcutta slum industries, 1974
(in Rs.)

Item	Amount per establishment	Amount per worker
(1)	(2)	(3)
Estimated value of :		
(i) machinery	10 000	1 470
(ii) land and buildings	5 900	855
Total fixed capital	15 900	2 325
(iii) working capital	14 200	2 075
Total productive capital	30 100	4 400

by these slum units which needed only Rs 4,400 worth of productive capital to employ one person even in the Calcutta area should be emphasised again. It may be mentioned that in the registered factory sector, only fixed capital per employee was more than Rs 15,000 in 1968 in India, i.e. more than six times that which prevailed in these slum units even in 1974.

Total outstanding loans for these units came to Rs 1,742,000 or Rs 2,648per unit. The distribution pattern by source of loan is presented in table 57. The average in the table do not reflect the reality properly. Firstly, loans from banks and Government were available to only a few units—but have been averaged over all the units. Secondly, information on loans from informal sources, particularly from private money lenders, more often than not, is not or cannot be divulged.

4.3. RESULTS FROM SOME CASE STUDIES OF SELECTED UNITS

The necessity for conducting selected case studies, as distinct from normal sample surveys, has been discussed at the beginn-

TABLE 57

Pattern of distribution of outstanding loan per unit by its source, Calcutta area slum industries, 1974

Source of loans	Amount of average outstanding loans per unit (in Rs.)	Percentage distribution
(1)	(2)	(3)
1. Bank	1 572	58.6
2. Government	269	10.0
3. Friends and relatives	476	17.7
4. Private money lender	174	6.5
5. Others	193	7.2
Total	2 684	100.0

ing of this chapter. Despite the relevance of the type of technology in these informal sector industries in a capital-scarce, labour-surplus country like India, the earners engaged in the informal sector units—both the wage workers as well as the owner-workers—remained relatively very poor, mainly because this sector had to depend, in a way, on the mercy of the few large houses controlling modern industry, often with unnecessarily very high capital intensity and, what is more important, controlling the marketing system. The nature of this organised sector is such that it has become an economic necessity with them to depend for their excessive profit on the poverty of the informal sector, and the overall domination of this organised sector over our whole economy is the basic economic reason for the continuation of poverty in the informal sector.

With very high capital cost, in terms of capital used per unit of output or per unit of employment, in large industry, along with relatively high wages which the organised workers could manage to get from these large houses, it would have been very difficult for them to sell their goods in the market if they were to produce all their goods, leading to very high cost of

7

production. One way to reduce that cost of production for the large producers is to make use of a technology with lower capital cost and lower wage rate, so that the over-all cost of production goes down. This is the reason why these large "producers" try more and more to have their goods produced cheaply in the informal sector. The benefit of this cheap cost of production, however, does not go either to the informal sector, or to the ultimate consumer. The existence of the large houses controlling the market ensures effectively that the informal sector producers hand over their produce to the organised sector for marketing the goods, they themselves have produced, under well-known, often internationally famous, brand names, at a far higher price. This "cost" of marketing often exceeds by far the total cost of production. This is the typical case of that part of the informal sector, which is modern, and produces—despite low capital intensity, low wages, unsophisticated factory shed, etc.—really skilled, sophisticated products which also often includes embossing the labels or trade marks of the other larger factory under whose name the product will ultimately be sold in the market. This also applies to those who produce significant parts or components which are then assembled by the larger producer or some other sub-contractor engaged by the larger "producer".

The other part of the informal sector may be called traditional and it produces cheap goods for the poorer section of the people. This poorer section of the people often does not generate an effective demand even for their daily need of food and so it is no wonder that they can demand only very few industrial goods, and that also only if the latter can be supplied at a low price. The traditional informal sector takes a leading role in supplying whatever few non-agricultural goods the poorer majority of our people can afford to demand. With this background, let us now look at a few typical cases.

In a slum at Fulbagan (central Calcutta—see table 48) we found a small family-based footwear manufacturer. Besides working himself, with help from other family members, the owner provided employment to four adults and two children aged about 12 to 14 years. This whole group of workers sits in a small room of about 120sq. ft. and manufactures, with a labour of eight hours per day, two dozen sophisticated sandals. The total wage bill for the six hired workers comes to Rs 16 per day, at the rate of Rs 8 per dozen, and this comes to an average wage of Rs 2.67 per day per worker which, at the 1974 price level in this part of India could fetch less than 1 kg. of rice in the open market. Because of this low wage and the informal way they produce the goods, it is possible for the owner to sell his goods wholesale at the rate of Rs 130 per dozen or about Rs 11 per pair of sandals to a very famous "producer" of shoes. Those sandals are then marketed by the "producer" under their brand name at a rate of Rs 22.95 per pair or Rs 275.40 per dozen. The gap between the price at which the actual producer sells his produce and the price at which the middleman—though formally known as a producer—sells them to the sophisticated consumer may be noted. This is the gap which separates the market of informal sector goods and the market where the formal sector sells those goods to the ultimate consumer.

In the same slum another footwear producer, employing four adults and one child, produces a more sophisticated variety of ladies' sandals. These are mainly of two types : one type is sold to the middleman at a price of Rs 17 or 18 per pair, the other type at a price of Rs 30 or 32 per pair. The "middleman" sells these two varieties from sophisticated shops in downtown Calcutta at a price of Rs 32 and Rs 72 per pair respectively. This unit produces about one dozen pairs of shoes per day. The wage is about Rs 5 per day.

A somewhat bigger producer unit in the same area, and employing about ten workers on a daily basis at Rs 5 per day, produces what is called the "hawain chappal". They supply this chappal at only Rs 15 to 18 per dozen to the wholesale traders who then arrange for their sale through retail agents at about Rs 60 per dozen. They could reduce further their cost of production, though most probably they would be unable to reap the benefit of the lower cost themselves. This cost reduction could have been achieved if the small producer could get raw materials needed by him at a controlled rate. For example, one of the essential requirements is titaniam at the rate of 125 kg. per month. They purchase it at Rs 30 per kg. while the actual controlled rate is Rs 7.50 per kg. Again, so far as rubber is concerned, of which their monthly requirement is 500 kg., they purchase it at Rs 10.50 per kg., while the controlled rate is only Rs 7.50 per kg. Again, as regards another item of raw material, viz. wax, their monthly requirement is only 150 kg. They purchase it at Rs. 3.50 per kg. while the controlled rate is Rs. 2.10 per kg. We find above the typical example of what is meant by operating in a different market so far as purchase of inputs is concerned. While the small producer can only go to the open or black market where the price is much higher, the large producers, who can easily have contacts with the authorities and can afford to maintain an organisation to establish such contacts, can get these raw materials at the actual controlled rate either through the Government or through the manufacturers.

We may now take up a really sophisticated small-scale engineering unit in south Calcutta. We give below the items they used to produce and sell to internationally-famous "producers" for their ultimate sale in the market. They used to produce butterfly flow control valves for pipelines with 18-inch cast iron bodies. They used to sell it at the rate of Rs 2,200 to the famous "producer" who then used to sell it in the market at a price of Rs 5,100 per unit. Moreover, the smaller unit used to supply his product on credit covering three months supply to the large producer. This meant that the working capital for the small producer was blocked reducing drastically the turnover of his capital, while the larger units required no additional working capital for purchasing the goods, thereby reducing drastically their own working capital need. This unit, as well as many other units which I had the occasion to visit, complained that the large producers often do not pay back the amount due within three months but take four or five months to pay the price of their produce. Another item they used to manufacture was a tapping machine which they used to sell to another very famous producer at Rs 1,300, minus 10 per cent discount, i.e. at Rs 1,170 per unit. The latter, however, used to sell it in the market at a price of Rs 1,875. A third item they used to produce is a 5 h.p. wheat thresher which they used to supply to another internationally-famous "producer" at Rs 850 per unit, while the latter used to market it to the peasants at a price of Rs 1,575. Another item, a 10 h.p. wheat thresher, also used to be supplied to the same big producer at a price of Rs 1,075, while the latter sold it to the peasants at Rs 2,200. Another item was a compressure sprayer which they used to supply also to this big concern at Rs 180 per piece while the latter sold it at Rs 250 per piece. We can see from the above examples a further confirmation that the market in which the small unit operates is very different from that in which the large unit operates and the mechanism of the relationship between the two markets is such that the latter market utilises the former markets for its own benefits. This unit also had to borrow from a private money lender an amount of Rs 70,000 at an interest rate of 27 per cent per year, i.e. about three times the then usual interest rate from the banks. This unit also provided us with an example as to how large units put additional burdens on the small units. Some three years back they were supplying goods to a famous "producer" who, by assuring them that they would purchase regularly goods from that unit, induced it to purchase a sophisticated capstan lathe at a price of Rs 70,000. Once the unit had been saddled with that heavy investment, the concerned large "producer" started to reduce the rate at which they were to purchase the output and ultimately refused to accept its goods. This units offers another example of a different type of manifestation of this difference in market. A big cigarette manufacturer used to import a cigarette rolling machine called "garniture" at a price of Rs 1,500 per unit in 1964. This internationally-famous tobacco goods manufacturer then sponsored one of its own subsidiaries to take advantage of the policy of import substitution to develop an India-made garniture which they then used to market at Rs 3,500 per unit in 1970/1971. The small unit which we have been studying started to manufacture exactly the same machine but because they did not have either a famous brand name or a control over the marketing organisation they had to sell it at a price of only Rs 2,000.

This takes us to another concern located in the northern suburb of the city producing "black tapes." The present owner-producer of "black tapes" was once the main technical man in a big concern and was responsible for developing the "black tape" which that organisation has been selling in the market. But when that same man produces exactly the same thing in a small unit under his own guidance, he is forced to compete with the produce of his one-time employer, which he himself developed, by offering a lower price and higher discount to the trader. This is another manifestation of difference in the market between a small producer and the large producer.

We can now take up another unit producing unsophisticated but not exactly traditional goods. It produces cycle seats in an unsophisticated fashion and sell these to smaller cycle shops at a very cheap price. This is a typical family shop where two adults and two juniors from the same family work. The work space consists of a small room of 130 sq. ft. with a rent of Rs 20 per month, and their sole equipment consists of a sewing machine rented at a cost of Rs 15 per month and a few scissors, knives, etc. Despite the heavy work of four members of the family for the whole day, their monthly income from this small enterprise hardly exceeds Rs 60. The income of this family is augmented by the head of the family who works as a hawker of cloth and earns daily about Rs 3. Another member of his family—a divorced sister—also earns Rs 1.80 per day by preparing paper packets at Rs 0.62 per thousand. A person working about eight to ten hours per day can produce 3,000 packets, providing an income of about Rs 1.80 per day. Thus, the monthly income of this family is about Rs 60+Rs 90+Rs 50 or Rs 200 per month. With this income they have to maintain 12 persons in the family providing a monthly expenditure per capita of only Rs 18. The society compels them to pay this price of semi-starvation in order that they may produce and sell cheap.

We may now take up another unit started in 1972 and which has very recently been wound up. They started with a capital of Rs 3,000 and were some sort of an ancillary to a medium producer. The working force consisted of three partner friends, all educated unemployed, together with one hired wage worker. Their fixed capital consisted of a small dilapidated all *kucha* shed of 150 sq. ft. in a small slum developed on a graveyard at Manicktolla (north-central Calcutta) for which they were not required to pay any rent, plus a used moulding machine which they obtained free from another friend (its price would have been Rs 600), and another smaller moulding machine, produced in the informal sector at Howrah, which they had to purchase at a price of Rs 400. In addition, they had four pairs of scissors worth Rs 20 and a few very small implements costing less than Rs 10. They used to produce washers and rubber rings worth about Rs 530 per week. Their input cost was about 140 per week, transport costs were Rs 10 per week, the wage of the only hired worker was Rs 30 per week, making the total cost of production something around Rs 180 per week, leaving a balance of Rs 350 minus Rs 180—i.e. Rs 170 per week for the three owner-workers, or Rs 56 per head per week as "profit" plus "wage". The three partners would have been quite satisfied with this income of Rs 56 per head per week if only other elements of "unusual" cost did not intrude to transform their income into loss leading to the winding up of the enterprise. It is the heavy burdens arising from those costs that are responsible for the high mortality amongst informal sector units, referred to in Chapter 3 while dealing with the CMPO Survey of 1962. Almost the sole purchaser of their goods was a medium unit which, in its turn, was an ancillary to the biggest car manufacturer in India. Extra incidental "informal" costs which this unit had to bear, in addition to the normal costs of input, wage, etc. referred to earlier, included (i) a regular bribe to the store in charge of the medium-scale company so that the goods supplied to them by the small unit were not rejected ; (ii) a regular bribe to the purchase officer for securing the order ; and (iii) a regular bribe to the accounts officer so that they might obtain payments for the goods supplied without much delay. Other types of extra cost, also typical to informal sector units, included : (i) as the unit did not have an electric power connection, they had to depend on an inefficient and high-cost coal press. An additional fact remained, however, as one of the partners explained to me : it was not possible for them to purchase a costly electric press costing about Rs 1,200 as they had no money ; (ii) absence of a power connection forced them to work without sufficient light which made the operations inefficient ; (iii) absence of capital forced them to purchase raw material from the retail market in small quantities, pushing up the cost of raw material by at least 20-25 per cent ; (iv) much less than full utilisation of tempo (small lorry) space, because of their smaller volume of production, meant very high cost of transport per unit of goods produced and delivered for sale. Despite all these difficulties, the unit managed to exist for more than one year, showing the extreme vitality of these informal sector units. They ultimately had to wind up when their main client—the medium unit—declared a lock-out without paying their debt of Rs 1,500. In the meantime they had already advanced Rs 500 for purchasing another moulding machine—indicating how eagerly these small units try to reinvest and expand—which was not finalised ultimately. Blocking of this capital made it impossible for the unit to function and they had to close down. This is a short history of birth and death of small units in the informal sector. Incidentally, this unit was not registered with the Directorate of Cottage and Small-Scale Industry.

Let us now take up another unit. This is a relatively modern unit supplying 85 per cent of its produce to an internationally famous electric and electronic goods manufacturer. Data from this unit regarding price differentials in the purchase of inputs are most instructive. Let us take up the items one by one : (i) as against the controlled price of cold rolled sheet of less than Rs 2,000 per ton, they purchase it at a price of Rs 5,000 to 5,500 per ton ; (ii) as against the controlled price of steel plate ranging from Rs 1,500 to 2,000 per ton, they purchase it at more than Rs 3,000 per ton ; (iii) they purchase aluminium sheet from the market at a price of Rs 23 per kg., while the large units purchase direct from the sheet manufacturer at a price of only Rs 13 per kg. The way the large "manufacturer" forced the unit to sell its goods at a low price may be evident from the fact that the rate at which they agreed to purchase street lighting fittings from the unit (Rs 25 per piece) in 1961 could not be raised up to 1971 despite about a three-fold increase in cost of input and labour during this period. It could also be learnt from the unit that the entire medical equipment and 50 per cent of the light fittings supplied under the brand name of the large "manufacturer" are actually manufactured by small units. The comparative price at which the small unit sold these to the large manufacturer and the price at which the later sells to the ultimate consumer is also instructive :

(i) light shed sold by the small unit at Rs 8.50 each, which was then sold by the large house at Rs 17 each ;

(ii) light fixture sold by the small unit at Rs 32 each, which was then sold by the large house at Rs 90 each ;

(iii) operation lamp sold by the small unit at Rs 3,500 each which was then sold by the large house at Rs 10,500 each.

The qualitative picture that emerges from these case studies fully confirms the hypothesis that the dominating large-scale oligopolistic sector compels the small unit in the informal sector to operate in a different market where the input price is higher and the output price is lower, and the main benefit of this price differential is reaped by the large-scale sector. It also confirms that whom we often call large industrial houses are, in effect, commercial in nature and earn a major part of their profit by trading goods produced by smaller units. But despite this relationship of, what may be called, exploitation between the large and the small units, the latter can exist, given the present socio-economic structure, only when they can get the opportunity of offering themselves to be "exploited" by the larger units. An understanding of this mutual dependence between the large and the small sector in our present-day society and the nature of this dependence is the starting point for developing a programme for the development of the informal sector, attempted in the last chapter.

The nature of the informal sector, including the dynamics of its functioning can, thus, never be understood in isolation by concentrating only on the informal sector. An understanding of the pattern of functioning of the overall economy and the role informal sector plays in it, is the pre-requisite for understanding the informal sector and for suggesting a programme for its desirable development in the interest of the poorer majority of the country.

4.4 Results from some Case Studies of Selected Slum Areas

Paikpara Bustee No. 13[1]

Bustee No 13 in Paikpara is a slum situated in the northern fringe of Calcutta. Out of 140 families residing in this area, 78 depend on trade and manufacturing of ready-made garments. These 78 families can be divided into three groups :

i) three medium traders who, along with 12 others living outside the slum area, control the main trade in this industry. They employ capital, owned or borrowed from a bank, provide facilities to workers by offering them working space, sewing machines and other implements and of course a piece-rate wage. They collect all the finished goods and then sell them at wholesale. This group belongs to the "formal sector", and is also organised in an Association which fixes wages and helps them to borrow capital from the organised capital market at relatively low interest rates.

ii) twenty five small traders. This group is to be distinguished from the earlier one, not only by the fact of their smallness but also by the very important fact that, along with trading, they and their family members do participate directly in the production process. They operate on the border line of the informal and formal sectors. They depend on private money lenders for working capital.

iii) the remaining 50 families depend upon wage income. They work either in their own home, sometimes with their own machine and more often with a machine hired from the medium traders @ Rs. 10/-to Rs 15/-per month, or in the shops with sewing machine, etc. set up by the traders and do whatever work is given to them. In the latter case, they are not required to pay the rent of the machine. They belong to the informal sector.

The workers in the third group above can be divided into several categories by the type of work they do. First comes the

1 The report on this slum has been prepared by Miss Tapati Kar Chaudhury, a social worker of CUSCON.

"cutters" who are relatively skilled people and work mainly on a part-time basis in shops and get paid on piece-rate terms. On an average, they are linked with two shops and earn about Rs 250 to Rs 300 per month. A few are more skilled and are attached to 3 or 4 shops and evidently they earn more.

Second comes the group engaged in machine sewing. These workers work on an average about 8 to 10 hours per day and sew 3 to 6 dozen garments, depending upon the kind of garments they are sewing. Despite wide variations in the piece-rate they get for different types of garments, their average earning remains more or less fixed round about Rs 100/-per month. There is a marked seasonal fluctuation in production. The peak is during autumn Puja festival (September-October) and at that time they earn more than Rs 150/-per month, working 12-14 hours per day. The slack season when there is not much work just follows the peak. Next comes the group who are engaged in hand-sewing. There is some element of finishing work in most of the garments which can best be done, of course, if the labour is cheap, by hand-sewing. This work includes piping, etc. The rate for this hand-sewing varies from Rs 1.25 to Rs 3/- per dozen. This work is mainly done by the women who are otherwise engaged in house work and do this work whenever they get some spare time. Allied to this group are those who are engaged in fitting buttons, etc. Normally a worker can fix buttons etc. to 1-3 dozen garments and earn Rs 1.50 to Rs 3/- per day. Their average monthly earning is about Rs 50/-per month.

The wage is very low and their bargaining position is very bad, particularly because, now, a large number of women in the slums in the neighbouring areas also want to take up such work and have been doing so. Thus, the poverty of these people itself, in a way, guarantees a low wage, and the latter in its turn makes it possible for the formal sector, the medium trader, to earn a good profit by trading the goods produced by these workers. It may be mentioned that in October 1974, these workers formed an organisation and launched a strike demanding, among other things, a higher rate of wage. But poverty and, following from it, lack of holding capacity, stood in the way of their success and the slum workers in this area failed to get their wage rate increased.

The economics of this informal sector garment industry is based on the cost differential between the "made to order" garments and relatively mass manufactured ready-made garments. This can be made clear with an example relating to making ladies blouses. For the "made to order" variety, an average blouse takes 0.75 metre costing Rs 3.23 for cloth at the rate of Rs 4.30 per metre in the retail market ; the tailoring charge, including cost of buttons, thread, etc. is Rs 3/-, so that the total cost of a blouse is Rs 6.23. So far as ready-made garments are concerned, they firstly save on cloth, thanks mainly to mass manufacture, and use only 0.63 metre, a saving of the order of 16 per cent. Then they save on the price differential between wholesale and retail. The cloth which is sold at Rs 4.30 per metre in the retail market, is sold at Rs 3.25 in the wholesale market, a price saving of 24 per cent. Lastly, they save on wage and incidental expense : while it was Rs 3.00 in the "made to order" variety, it was only Rs 0.36 (wage)+0.14 (cost of thread, etc.)+0.20 (establishment cost) or only Rs 0.70 in the case being studied, denoting a saving of 76 per cent. It must, however, be said that a large part of these savings benefit the ultimate consumer, the less sophisticated and poorer consumers, because our wholeseller sells this blouse at only Rs 3.00 and the ultimate consumer in the retail market gets it at a price of about Rs 3.50 to Rs 4.50 depending upon the location of the shop. The total cost of a blouse being Rs 2.70, composed of cloth at Rs 2.0J and wage and other incidental charge at Rs 0.70 the wholeseller earns a profit of Rs 0.30 per blouse, which is about 83 per cent of the wage. Thus, if our informal sector slum worker could get a loan, say, from the bank for purchasing a sewing machine and for some working capital, and if he had direct access to the market, then he could have had earned Rs 0.66 per blouse, instead of the Rs 0.36 which he earns to-day. This increase in earning could have meant for this slum worker crossing the poverty line and hence, a qualitative change in his mode of existence.

The small traders, however, cannot earn profits at the rate

described above. Unlike the medium and large traders, these small traders have to rely on loans from private money lenders at a rate of 120 per cent per annum. Because of this high cost of capital, they are forced to operate with far less than an optimum amount of capital. Hence, they often cannot get the benefit of purchasing inputs on a large scale, and they are forced to take a relatively smaller quantum of goods to the market, increasing thereby the transport cost per unit of output. Moreover, the small traders who are also workers, cannot procure sufficient material to keep them engaged throughout the week. What, however, is more important is the fact that the small traders cannot stock a sufficient amount of output before the busy season of the October festival, and so cannot, unlike the large traders with higher holding capacity with cheaper credit, make best use of the good market during October. They, however, try to make good a part of the enormous disadvantage they suffer by approaching the retail market directly as street hawkers. Their mode of working, their income level etc. make them an integral part of the informal sector economic activity in the slum area.

The plight of these people can be illustrated with some individual case studies. One widow with five additional dependents (one sister and four daughters) owns a second-hand machine, purchased for Rs 210 only two years back out of the fund she received from the employer of her husband when he died. The machine requires constant repair and she had so far spent Rs 40/- on it. All the six persons live in a "room" of about 60 sq. ft. and there also she works throughout the day sewing 3 dozens of garments. Her earning varies from Rs 16 to Rs 20 per week, i.e. less than Rs 0.50 per head per day. This income is supplemented by a very uncertain income of plastic bag packing at the rate of Rs 0.10 per kg. If she could own another machine, her sister could also then work and thereby increase the per capita daily income to nearly Rs 1.00. Even this income is far below the poverty line. Still this is the dream she dreams.

Unlike the above family where only one person, in the main, can work with the machine, there is a family of six of whom three—the wife and the two daughters—are engaged in hand sewing. The husband and the adult son are unemployed. The three together sew per day three dozens of frocks at Rs 1.20 per dozen and 2 dozens of blouses at Rs 1.20—1.50 per dozen. Thus, their income per day is about Rs 6.00, or Rs 1.00 per capita per day, despite the fact that half of the family are earners. They are dreaming about purchasing a sewing machine, or at least hiring it. The reality is as yet far from the dream.

There is another family where almost every one works. The family is composed of a widow and her three sons and one daughter. The eldest son sews with a machine in a shop and earns, with 8-10 hours hard work, about Rs 7.00 per day, and gets work for 5 days a week. The method of payment of wage is interesting. He gets Rs 25.00 per week (during October, Rs 50.00 per week when he works 12-18 hours a day) as an advance every week. At the end of the year, the annual account is cleared and if it is found that he has overdrawn, then he must pay back by working without wage. He also gets a small commission of 12 per cent of the wage he earns. His younger brother (age 13 years) works at home with a sewing machine which they had purchased for Rs 300 out of their past savings when their father died 6 years back. He works 8-10 hours a day sewing plain pettycoats and earns Rs 4.20 by sewing 7 dozens of such pettycoats. His sister (age 9 years) is engaged in hand sewing of blouses and earns Rs 1.50 per day. The average weekly income of the family is about Rs 70/- or Rs 1.70 per capita per day. The main dream of the eldest brother is to learn well the art of cutting and sewing trousers and jackets etc. and get a job with a higher wage in a medium tailoring shop manufacturing "made to order" garments.

Tapsia Bustee[1]

Tapsia Bustee is a slum area on the eastern fringe of Calcutta by the side of the open canal which carries the major part of the sewage and drainage outflow from the Calcutta urban area for its final disposal in the rivers of south 24-Parganas. There are a large number of tanneries in this area ; but rather than tanneries, the industries dealing with rubber goods (Hawaii

1. The report on this slum has been prepared by Mr Wazed Ali, a social worker of CUSCON.

chappals etc.) are linked with the livelihood pattern of the slum dwellers in this slum. There are about 60 rubber goods manufacturing units in this area, of which 50 per cent are relatively large employing about 20 workers, and the remaining 50 per cent are small employing less than 10 workers. They put out a large part of their work to the family members of the slum dwellers at the rate of about 20-35 families per productive unit. In that way about one thousand slum-dwelling families in Tapsia are indirectly employed by this rubber industry.

The main work done by the family labour is the finishing of straps for rubber sandals. They get about Rs 0.10 per dozen and they can finish about 15-20 dozens by working throughout the day. In this way they can earn about Rs 2/- per day per person. Because of their poverty-stricken condition, they are forced to take this near starvation wage. Since they have no better alternative, even this starvation wage is a boon to them.

One important aspect of this industry, like many other industries, is severe competition between the smaller units and the larger ones. The larger units with better complement of machinery etc. can produce goods with better finish and so they reach a better market in good shops in good areas in the formal sector. The smaller units, because of their poor finish, can have a market only in the so-called informal sector trading activities, i.e. in the pavement shops where low quality cheaper goods are sold to relatively poorer people.

The smaller units suffer also owing to lack of credit. The goods are sold in this area with credit of 2 to 3 months. It becomes very difficult for the small units to wait for this period. Because of a chronic shortage of working capital, they cannot purchase raw materials at the wholesale rates and cannot avail themselves of the seasonal fluctuations in the raw material prices. For example, in 1974, raw material for the industry was sold at Rs 800 per tonne in the rainy season and this price shot up to Rs 1,400 per tonne in the winter. The larger units, because of their easy command over working capital, could stock the raw material when it was cheap, but the smaller units could not take advantage of this opportunity. The smaller units cannot purchase some of the costly machines, and therefore, they have to depend on the larger unit for some parts and have to pay relatively higher prices to these units for these items.

The smaller productive units can improve their condition materially if they can have an assured supply of working capital and also term loans at a rate of interest prevailing in the organised market.

The informal sector producing units, mostly incapable of availing themselves of the facilities of the organised market, have to balance the relatively higher cost of inputs and of capital, by incurring lower wage cost, on the one hand, and by depending on the pavement market for the poorer people, on the other. These units, thus, are based on poverty and also serve the poor.

*Tiljala area Bustee**

Tiljala is a slum in the eastern fringe of Calcutta, one of the most backward areas of this city. In the survey conducted in this slum area in 1975, it was found that of the earners in this area, 24 are rickshaw-pullers, 28 are vendors of vegetables and fish, 12 are working as servants in different house-holds, 244 are engaged in the building industry, 50 are washermen, 16 are vendors of other goods, 15 are small traders, 9 work in some organised office, 9 work in the tanning industry, 10 work in the small units for manufacturing musical toys, and the remaining 71 work in various other fields.

The environmental sanitation condition here is appalling. Despite the fact that about 190 sanitary latrines were constructed in the area two years back, due to extremely bad maintenance, these have become, rather than a source of help in this area, a source of positive nuisance.

This report takes up only one trade in this area i.e. the manufacture of musical toys, which is a hereditary cottage industry in this area. As a matter of fact, a specific part of this slum is named after these musical toys.

The main problem of this industry is the absence of adequate

* This report has been prepared by Miss Arati Sanyal, a social worker of CUSCON.

working capital. The rate of return over investment is quite high. As a matter of fact, while the cost of an average item ranges from Rs 1.00 to Rs 1.50 per toy, its sale price varies from Rs 1.75 to Rs 2.50. Thus the rate of return on the unit sold is quite high and is about 70 per cent. However, as they can sell only a few items due to paucity of working capital, the absolute amount earned by these people is small. Moreover, as they themselves have to go out to sell the goods, they lose the day's production when they do so. If they had more money, they could engage another man for selling the goods and then they could have utilised the time in producing more goods.

A part of these toys use near-wastes of the tannery industry nearby, and utilise this industry, which otherwise is a big source for creating environmental insanitation, for a positive purpose.

Some help with bank finance, with technical guidance for achieving a better finish, and direct accessibility to the organised formal sector market, could move them from below the poverty line to above the poverty line. But this is still far beyond even their wild dreams.

Ramlilabagan, Cossipore[1]

Ramlilabagan is a slum in Cossipore in the northern part of Calcutta. There are about 800 families in this slum of whom about 100 depend on carpentry. All these carpenter families have been carrying on this trade in a hereditary fashion. The carpenter families can be divided into three groups :

1) the families who are simultaneously manufacturers and traders. They have a small place where they work and display their goods.
2) the carpenters who work with their own tools and in their own home on daily piece-rate wage basis on orders from different concerns.
3) informal co-operatives, each with 4 or 5 carpenters who operate from a single house where they manufacture the

1 This report has been prepared by Miss Sunanda Munshi, Mr Monoj Dey, Mr Arunava Maity and Miss Tapati Kar Chaudhury, all social workers of CUSCON.

goods on order, or on their own and then arrange for their sale.

The first group, e.g. the trader-cum-manufacturers, operate in two fashions ;

i) they take orders from the organised big shops from the furniture market located mainly at the central business district of Calcutta. As per the work order from the formal sector, our slum units in the informal sector invest their own money to purchase raw material and manufacture the goods with their own labour sometimes aided by hired labour. They deliver the goods in an unpolished fashion to those big shops and the latter then take up the work of polishing with their own employees. One of the main difficulties of these small trader-cum-manufacturers is that they do not have much capital and, apart from depending on relatives, they are forced to take loans from the private money lenders ; a large part of the income therefore leaks out as interest charges to the money lenders. The rate of interest prevailing in this area is abnormally high. They take loan of Rs. 30 with an interest charge of Rs. 1 per day, and they are to pay back this money with interest within 2 months 12 days. (The imputed interest rate comes to 1218 per cent per year !) They do not keep any regular wage worker in their shops. Whenever there is need they hire the workers on a daily basis at Rs. 8 to Rs. 12 per day depending upon the nature of the work. The economics of their operation may be clear from the following example :

Cost of manufacturing wooden almirah (size 5 ft. x 3 ft. x 1½ ft.) :

a)	wage	Rs. 30
b)	materials	Rs. 160
c)	transport and miscellaneous	Rs. 5
d)	interest on Rs. 150 for 3 days	Rs. 15
		Rs. 210

They deliver this almirah to the big shops at Rs 220 making a profit of Rs 10 excluding their imputed wage income. Normally it takes about three days if the owner himself manufactures it with his own labour. It may be noted that if he could get credit from a bank even at a 15 per cent rate of interest per year, his interest cost would have been only Rs 0.20, instead of what he actually is forced to pay, viz. Rs 15.00. This would have had increased his profit, other things remaining the same, from Rs 10 to Rs 24.80 per almirah, which is nearly the same rate at which shops in the organised sector get profit. Low profitability of these small units, thus, arises not so much from their smallness as such but from the operation of a socio-economic force which condemns them to operate in a different market where amongst other things, the rate of interest is more than 1200 per cent per year. The big shop, after getting delivery of the unpolished almirah, spends about Rs 70 on polishing material, wages, etc., so the total cost to the big shop comes to Rs 290 (excluding overheads in the shops). They sell the almirah to the consumer at Rs 320-350, making a gross profit of Rs 30 to Rs 60 per almirah. Thus the lion's share of the profit goes to the big shops in the formal sector, while the small trader-cum-manufacturer perhaps earns an income which cannot take him appreciably above the poverty line.

ii) The second way through which these small trader-cum-manufacturers work is by taking orders from the direct consumer. Normally some of the consumers, who know these traders personally, advance them money against their order. It is, therefore, more beneficial to work in this fashion because the problem of working capital is to a large extent solved through this mechanism. But they do not get adequate orders of this sort.

Next we may take up the second group of workers who work on a daily rate basis. They normally take orders from bigger shops who advance them raw materials and they then take these raw materials home and work there with their own instruments. They get wages on a piece-rate basis, and this rate is much lower than what a worker gets in an organised formal sector shop : for example, they get about Rs 6 for manufacturing one "bracket" while a regular worker in a big shop gets just double this sum for manufacturing the same item. These informal sector workers, however, get work more or less throughout the year, and earn an income of about Rs 200 per month.

The third group consists of four or five informal cooperatives each with about 5 workers. Each unit has one room where they work together with their own instruments, and carry out orders which they receive from different shops or directly from the consumers. They divide up the sales proceeds amongst themselves as per the work done by each, and the man who collects the specific order gets a little extra. There is a lot of benefit in the way they manufacture in a co-operative fashion. As they work together, the pressure for mobilising capital is reduced to some extent and because a group works together they can collect bigger orders and hence they get more work.

Though the work of carpenters is not seasonal, yet there is some slackening of work during the monsoon due to the difficulty they face in storing their goods in the open, which obviously is the normal storage place in this part of the world.

Most of these carpenters try to manufacture some items, when there is no specific order, which they sell either directly or through some hawker. Normally these are cheap goods and are sold through pavement shops.

The general condition of these carpenters may be made clearer by referring to some specific cases. First, let us take up a family consisting of 9 persons, (husband, wife, and 7 children) ; this is apart from a daughter who has already been married. The carpenter worked as a piece-rate worker for 7 years, and then for the last 13 years in his own small shop. For the shop, he took a space at a rent of Rs 30 per month and then he had to renovate the space by spending Rs 1900. In addition, he spent Rs 200 for implements. Thus, his total fixed capital cost was only Rs 2,100 which he could invest in five years. He gets regular orders not only from Calcutta city proper but also from the suburbs. As he has not much working capital, he cannot engage wage workers and so he cannot accept all the 'orders'. In the last 13 years, only twice could he engage one man for some periods. Now he earns about Rs 300 per month or Rs 1.10 per capita per day for the family. This man dreams of getting a loan of Rs 5,000 at an interest rate prevailing in the organised market and engaging six additional workers at Rs 7 per day. He thinks that if somehow this could happen, then he could earn a reasonably good income even after providing a relatively good wage to those wage earners.

Next we take up a piece rate worker who has to support a family of six, including himself, with his own earning. He earns about Rs 35 per week or Rs 0.83 per capita per day. Apart from doing piece work against specific work he also manufactures small items on his own and sells them direct to pavement shops. He also earns some income by selling saw dust. The dream of this man also is to get a loan of Rs 3,000 at the organised market rate, and set up a small shop of his own.

The last case concerns an informal co-operative of five carpenters. Of these five persons, the oldest is 65 years old, the remaining four are in the age group 35-40 years. The average income of each of these carpenters is about Rs 135 per month. Each of them has invested about Rs 100 for purchasing instruments. They sell all their goods through hawkers and they themselves never go out to sell their goods. They get work throughout the year.

These carpenters, and also other carpenters, complained very much about the rapid rise of price of different tools and raw materials required in this carpentry business during the last 3 or 4 years. On enquiry from them it appears that during the period 1970/71 to 1975 the price rise of the different items was of the order of 200 to 300 per cent.

Phulbagan, Entally[1]

Phulbagan, Entally is a slum in the central Calcutta area

1 This report has been prepared by Miss Debasree Ghatak, Miss Anjana Guha and Mr Suptilal Basu.

which is bustling with industrial activity. The most important industry in this slum is shoe making. The workers in this ndustry have been engaged in this trade for generations and the work is highly specialised. No single unit manufactures all the components of a shoe. Each of them specialises in preparing one or more components and a few of course assemble these to manufacture the complete shoe. In this specialisation, however, the poorer people suffer. But as the small owner cannot purchase the machine, he has to get his polishing done by a relatively well-to-do unit in the same slum. While the latter gets Rs 8 for polishing one dozen soles, his worker who polishes it gets less than Rs 1.50 per dozen. Similarly, a relatively well-to-do owner having a leather spray and leather printing machine gets Rs 5 to Rs 8, depending on the nature of design, per foot of leather ; the worker actually doing this work gets only Rs 2 to Rs 2.50. And the price these slum units, taken as a whole, get from the large traders in the formal sector has been dealt with earlier in the discussion of specific case studies.

The extremely sophisticated specialisation of work in the shoe industry in this slum is to be seen to be believed. Thus, there are seven different types of soles manufacturer : leather sole, crepe sole, board sole, sponge sole, calf sole, rubber sole and tyre sole. Then, there are those engaged in manufacturing shoe belts and straps, wooden heels, leather spray and leather printings etc.

A large part of the women in this slum are engaged in manufacturing shoe-belts and straps. They get Rs 1.00 for sewing and Rs 0.10 for finishing 100 straps and, on an average, one worker can manage 1200 straps per day. They can earn per month, after paying the rent at Rs 20 per sewing machine per month, about Rs 300.

The reasons for concentration of these industries in this particular slum may be summarised as (i) availabilty of various types of skilled workers at one place, (ii) possibility of manufacturing all the parts in nearby household units, (iii) space required for manufacturing a specific component being small, possibility of accomodating it in household and small units, (iv) minimal transport cost for bringing together different parts, (v) availability of raw materials nearby, (vi) existence of some arrangement for marketing within the slum, and (vii) availability of cheap labour.

There are three different categories of entrepreneurs in this slum. These are: (i) very small units, with some cheaper implements only who take orders for and supply some specific components; (ii) relatively richer people owning several machines who earn an income only by hiring out these machines and whose rate of earning on invested capital is about 40 per cent; and (iii) relatively richer owners of machines engaged directly in manufacture by hiring some wage workers.

Some other linked industries have also grown up in this slum on the basis of the shoe industry. These are: (i) *stove washers* manufactured from cutting wastes of ordinary leather. These washers are available at the rate of about Rs 30 per quintal. For manufacturing washers, only one wooden hammer and one die are required. These washers are sold at the rate of Rs 200 per 144 pieces. The workers engaged in this trade earn about Rs 2.50 per day; (ii) *umbrella washers* manufactured from cutting wastes of calf leather. Implements required and earning are same as above; (iii) *cycle pedal covers* manufactured from cutting wastes of sole rubber. Implements required are wood and iron hammer, die and oven.

While all the three linked industries noted above are located in this slum, a fourth one noted below is not located here: (iv) what remains of the wastes after being used in the above three industries is sold at Rs 30 per quintal to traders who re-sell the wastes to units engaged in manufacturing organic manure.

Kumartolly[1]

Kumartolly is the site of the famous image makers situated in the north-western part of Calcutta. After Calcutta was born and became the seat of British rule in this part of the country, many big landlords lived in this emerging city. They brought the first group of image makers from the neighbouring district of Nadia and settled them at this spot, in order to get images

1. This report has been prepared by Sri Amitava Basu, a social worker of CUSCON.

of worship manufactured for them. In all probability the area got its present name from this fact of settlement of potters ("Kumar" in Bengali) in this area some 200 years ago.

With the spread of community worship, mainly because it was not possible to bear the associated high cost for a single individual or a single family, the demand for images rose rapidly And so starting with a few potters, this area now has about 160 shops in which about 600 potters work during the peak season before October. A part of these potters are permanently settled at Kumartolly and the rest (about 80 per cent) come to work here from their residences in the outlying districts where they work at other times as potters or sometimes as agriculturists.

About 50 per cent of these potters can take up any work connected with image making, while the others know well only one or two specific items of work. This latter group often work as "helpers" or "trainees". Each of these 160 shops keeps at least one such helper during the peak season. After spending 3 to 4 years as apprentices, they become full-fledged skilled image makers.

Even a few years back, all these potters belonged to specific potter's caste. However, now a few from other castes, including Brahmins, have taken up this profession.

Of these 160 shop owners, 30 are refugees from former East Pakistan. Leaving aside about 10 big shops, all the others are not in a good shape, particularly from financial point of view. The ten big shop owners get bank finance and they more or less dominate the market. The others mostly never could get a bank loan. A few of them who could manage to get some bank loans mostly failed to repay. The latter, numbering about 30, are medium sized shops. Thus, 120 small shops depend wholly on private money lenders, 30 medium sized ones depend partly on private money lenders and partly on banks, and the remaining 10 big shop owners are either able to finance themselves from their own savings or get the required loans from the banks.

Wages vary widely depending on the nearness of the peak period (October). The initial work, which requires the service of carpenters also, starts sometime in May and at that time the wage rate per man-day is, including food, about Rs 8 per day on an average. Around this average there is evidently variations depending upon the skill of the worker. This wage rate increases to about Rs 12 in August, and in September-October, it often exceeds Rs 20 per man-day, with a working day often exceeding 12-14 hours.

Raw material cost (wood, bamboo, straw, twine, rice husks, special clay, cloth, paints, etc.) for manufacturing one image of goddess Durga (8 ft. high) along with other accompanying images, comes to about Rs 300. Wage cost is about Rs 100. It takes about 7 to 10 man-days to manufacture such an image. So far as the small and medium shop keepers are concerned, their main constraint is lack of working capital. Due to its paucity, not only do they fail to manufacture a larger number of images, they are forced to have more concentrated work just before the festival, when the wage cost is relatively higher and the more skilled workers have already been engaged by others. This makes their cost of production higher and quality of produce often relatively inferior leading to a lower price of their product.

4.5. Conclusion

These area-wise case studies bring to the fore one aspect which did not come out so clearly in the unit-wise studies, viz., the possibility and necessity of undertaking an economic relief programme. Such a relief programme will not certainly bring about a basic change in the livelihood pattern of the urban poor in general and the slum poor in particular. But it can certainly initiate a change in some selected areas, a change which may convince them about the possibility of realising in practice a far bigger dream if they can somehow organise themselves.

The main content of this relief will not be providing them with some "free" money, a grant or even a loan at a differential rate of interest fixed for the poor. The conventional relief measures fail to understand that the poor man in the informal sector suffers because, for example, he cannot get a bank loan and he is forced to borrow often at a rate exceeding 10 times the interest rate charged by the bank. The basic dream of this man is not so much to get a loan at an interest rate lower than that normally charged by the banks, but an adequate loan at a rate at which the organised sector gets bank loans. Rather than providing some special help (such as a grant, an interest free loan, etc.), the question mainly is removing the prevailing discrimination against the poor in the informal sector which forces them to purchase at a higher price and sell at a lower price, compared to those in the organised fo rmal sector.

CHAPTER V

WHAT AILS THE METROPOLITAN ECONOMY

5.1. THE HISTORICAL ROOTS

THE BIRTH and development of the economy of metropolitan Calcutta are integrally linked up with the intrusion of the British East India Company into India in the seventeenth century and its subsequent political and economic subjugation of the country by the eighteenth century. The interests of British rule over India, and their variation over decades in response to the changing national and international situation, were the most dominant reality in shaping the economic structure of Calcutta in her pre-independence days, and it seems to have put an indelible mark on its functioning even now.

With independence, ultimate control over the Calcutta economy now lies in India—certainly the most important prerequisite for the re-emergence of a self-reliant and healthy informal sector but not in itself sufficient for starting a total developmental process which would inevitably embrace the small-scale, informal sector also. Basically the same pattern of relationship between the Calcutta metropolis and its vast hinterland, established during British rule and in the interest of that British rule, has continued even in the post independence days. Despite a basic change in the relationship between the Calcutta metropolis and the London metropolis, there has not occurred any basic change in the relation beteween the Calcutta metropolis and its rural and semi-rural hinterland.

The essence of this relationship between the Calcutta metropolis and its vast rural hinterland may become clear if we remember the way founding fathers of Calcutta, the British East India Company, solved their initial profound problem of trade between Bengal and Great Britain, namely, how to pay for the goods they wanted to take away from Bengal. They did not then have much in the way of goods themselves that Bengal was prepared to take in exchange. Neither was the mercantile company willing to part with gold and silver in exchange for Indian goods. The solution to their problem was the political subjugation of Bengal, and immediately raising the land revenue. That land revenue, which the Company as the ruler then owned, was used to "purchase" local goods for exporting abroad. This one-way transaction, by which one country could get goods from another country without the necessity of sending any goods or gold in exchange, was the starting point of the establishment of Calcutta as the seat of power, of foreign rule over India, and, through this power, also as the place for effecting the one-way transaction of goods.

The last year in the pre-British Indian rule in this part of the country was 1764/65. Total realisation of land revenue that year from Bengal was £817, 533. In the first year of the East India Company rule, 1765/66, it was increased to £1,470,000. By 1771/72, it was £2,441,000. When Lord Cornwallis imposed the permanent settlement in 1793, he fixed it at £3,400,000. How this rapidly rising land revenue helped to solve the basic problem of "trade" of the then ruling British East India Company is clear from the fact that during the first three years of direct British rule in India, mainly over Bengal, Bihar and Orissa, an export of goods worth £6,311,250 was achieved through an import of goods worth only £624,375 i.e. less than 10 per cent of what was exported mainly from the rural hinterland of Eastern India. While this type of trade provided the initial base for primitive accumulation or primary accumulation for the industrial revolution in Britain, its reverse side, negative accumulation, started to operate in India. And both the processes were cumulative.

It is not intended to trace here the different phases of development of the then ruling metropolis, London, and the United Kingdom, and the consequent phases of underdevelopment imposed on this colonial hinterland. What is emphasised here, with some examples of the pattern of relationship existing in its crudest form in the initial days of British rule over India, is that the essence of the colonial relation was an unequal exchange of goods leading to the withdrawal not only of the entire surplus but also of the substantial part of what would otherwise have been used for subsistence in the colonies, in the interest of the type of development strategy then pursued for the development of the metropolitan country. An understanding of the essence of this relationship and its necessary consequences particularly for India was the starting point for the design by the Indian nationalist movement of a proper development strategy which would use the income and employment potential of the colony for the benefit of the then colonial people themselves. The central focus of the strategy in India was the struggle for independence. Its necessary complement was utilising all other national activities, from the national education movement to the starting of Indian factories or even of capital-labour strikes within India, for strengthening and furthering the central aim, viz. a basic change in the then existing relation between the United Kingdom and India, i.e. between the metropolis and its colony.

The above points have been stated because they provide us with an understanding both of the historical base of the construction of independent India as well as of a developmental model with a marked relevance even today under very different circumstances.

What was the basis of the Calcutta metropolitan economy when the British had to leave India in 1947? Even in 1951, when India was declared a republic and the planning process of independent India had already been initiated, the economic scene of Calcutta was dominated, in the industrial sphere, by jute mills, and in the commercial sphere, by the export of jute goods and tea. All these activities, as we know, made Calcutta the jewel of what was then the British Empire, and accorded to it and to West Bengal, through the statistical process of averaging an external aura of development. None of our developmental strategists suspected at the time that what we then called signs of development, such as a larger proportion of "industries" in the Calcutta area, the larger volume of goods exported through Calcutta port, etc., might have been more appropriately conceived of as burdens of severe underdevelopment, rather than signs of development. It is this lack of understanding that lay at the root of the pursuit of a developmental effort which, instead of really developing West Bengal and the Calcutta metropolis, had further entrenched the burdens of underdevelopment, inherited from India's colonial past, and the crisis in the Calcutta metropolitan economy which is apparent today is an inevitable consequence of pursuing this wrong understanding and wrong policy.

It seems that we are becoming conscious about one aspect of this wrong understanding. This is expressed in the criticism, now being increasingly voiced particularly in West Bengal, of those regional development policies pursued by the Central Government which denied West Bengal and the Eastern states their locational advantage arising from proximity to coal and steel by adopting the policy of price equalisation of steel throughout India and telescopic freight rates for coal. This was a logical step from considering West Bengal as an industrially-developed state. Instead of further developing an already developed state, it was desirable in the interest of the country as a whole, so the Central Government argued, to help developing "backward states" by making available basic inputs to industry at the same or nearly the same price throughout India. It was not considered logically necessary to pursue the same policy with respect to other industrial raw materials, like cotton, oil seed, etc., which West Bengal had to bring from other states, because providing additional incentives to "already industrially-developed West Bengal and the Calcutta metropolis" were not necessary for achieving balanced regional development. The increasing volume of very just criticism against this regional development policy pursued by the Centre, particularly because its net result was to concentrate new industrial development not in backward areas but in some other "already developed States" is still now missing the central problem responsible for the malady in West Bengal and is, hence, fighting only against some specific manifestation of this malady, rather than against its central cause.

The basic weakness of these partial criticisms becomes clear from the way these critics advocate the need for industrial development *in general* in West Bengal by pointing out how it was thwarted by the policy pursued by the Centre; it is seldom that they refer explicitly to the *type* of industrial development required in West Bengal and the *type* of socio-economic structure required to carry it out. It is the realisation that what used to be called industrial development and metropolitan development in West Bengal were in effect the root cause of, and also the expression of, underdevelopment of this part of the country that underlies the policy objectives proposed here: a basic reorientation and restructuring of the present metropolitan industrial commercial base and then strengthening that restructured base, rather than further strengthening the existing metropolitan industrial commercial base and its structure.

What was, and is still, the basic requirement of functioning of the Calcutta metropolitan economy? The essence of it was to get raw jute for its industry and food for its people—both of which are obtained from the countryside. But what did this metropolitan economy produce, directly or indirectly, which could be exchanged against those rural goods? A perusal of these questions would inevitably lead us to the problems the East India Company faced in its trade with Bengal and the way they solved it.

The fundamental fact about the present structure of the rural economy is its extremely low productivity. At the current level of productivity, even if all the cultivated land in West Bengal were put under food production only, it could not satisfy the full hunger for food even of its own rural population, even if the entire food crop (excluding 10 per cent required for seed and normal wastage) were made available to the peasants. At the present level of productivity, it could make available, on those assumptions, about 8·5 million tonnes of food grain. This could provide to the present 40 million rural people (including their family members) of West Bengal, less than 600 grams of rice and wheat, which cannot even supply the minimum calorie requirement to the peasants, not to speak of a balanced diet. Under such a situation of productivity, if the peasants were free to consume whatever they produced, would there be any food surplus supporting the nearly 13 million urban population ? Would any jute or non-food crop be produced to feed the jute mills and other agro-based industries ?

The problem which such low productivity agriculture poses to the non-agricultural sector can be solved basically in two ways. One way is for the industrial sector to produce such inputs whose use in agriculture can increase its productivity more than proportionately, a part of which they may exchange against industrial inputs. With such a starting point, industry first operates as the basic tool for increasing agricultural productivity, with mutually beneficial terms of exchange between industry and agriculture, and then the high-productivity, high-income agriculture creates both the possibility of and need for, a gradually increasing volume of industrially produced consumption goods. In this model, initial industrial input for agriculture leading to generation of a real agricultural surplus (i.e. after meeting the full food requirement of the rural, peasant population), both in terms of food as well as in terms of agricultural raw materials, creates the basis for simultaneous, mutually-benefiting expansion of both agriculture and industry, as well as both rural and urban areas. This model could not possibly be followed in colonial India, and unfortunately it was not followed even in independent India.

The other way out of the problem arising from low productivity is to develop a mechanism of "forced saving" in agriculture and then to channel it to the urban, industrial sector without any necessity for paying the "forced savers". The earliest of such "peaceful" mechanisms was land revenue and rent. High land revenue and rent, based as they were on concentration of land ownership, nourished and strengthened the allied institutions of usury, rack renting and speculative commerce which in turn increased further the quantum of "forced saving" and led to further concentration of land ownership. All these institutions were successful from the point of view of generating a forced surplus for the urban, non-agricultural economy, in the over-all framework of a colonial economy which gradually decreased employment opportunities in industry both absolutely and relatively and concentrated the only other means of production in fewer and fewer hands. The industries encouraged by the colonial regime were jute, plantations and mining and an engineering industry for handling repairs, production of spare parts for those industries, heavy structurals and equipment required to keep the port and transportation operational. None of these industries was in any way concerned with supplying inputs to agriculture for increasing its productivity. This colonial industrialisation and urbanisation could, therefore, survive only if the producing peasants could be made to hand over to the urban sector, without demanding any goods in exchange, the produce which they themselves would have had otherwise consumed to satisfy their hunger. The mechanism of contriving this "peacefully" was zamindary and rack renting, under which actually working, producing peasants were forced to hand over 50 per cent of their meagre gross produce to the landowner, who was more often than not living in urban areas. A complementary process was usury, under which the peasants in the lean season took loans, either in cash or in kind, to be repaid often with more than 100 per cent rate of interest to the money lender—an efficient mechanism for generating forced surplus. The third aspect, speculative commerce, operated on the basis of distress sale of the peasants at a low price as soon as the crop was cut, or through the mechanism of *dadan* (advance purchase) by which the crop was sold at a very low price almost at the time it was sown. This third aspect was further reinforced by hoarding.

The role these institutions play may be made clear by contrast with a situation in which each peasant household will have an equal amount of land and none of them will have a rent or usurious loan burden. In such a situation an average peasant household, with six persons in the family, and with the present land availability in West Bengal, will own and work a 2.5 acre plot of land, and it will produce per annum, at the present average level of productivity, 15 quintals of rice/wheat. Deducting 2 quintals for seed and other input, the family will have a net annual output of 13 quintals or 217 Kg. per capita per year. If this entire output could be consumed by peasants as food grains, even then it will assure them only about 594 grams per capita per day, which can provide about 2,100 calories, i.e. less than the minimum average requirement of 2,500 calories. There would be no or negligible marketable surplus of food for non-peasants or production of jute, etc. for urban factories.

If this owner-cultivator of 2.5 acres of land can be made landless, then that family will earn, with its 1.5 workers getting work for 180 days in a year at an average wage of Rs 5 per man-day, only Rs 1350 per year or Rs 225 per capita per year. Even if 100% of this income can be spent on foodgrains, this can assure the family only 120 kg. of rice/wheat per capita per year, i.e. not more than 330 grams per capita per day. Thus, this transformation of an owner-cultivator into a landless agricultural labourer generates a "surplus" of 594-330 or 264 grams per person per day in the landless agricultural family. Remembering that 45 per cent of the peasants in West Bengal are landless, these 2.25 x 6 = 13.50 million persons in the landless agricultural worker's families in West Bengal now generate an annual "surplus" of 13.5 x 264 × 365 million grams or 1.3 million tonnes per annum. Were they not landless, this surplus would not have arisen.

Similarly if the owner-cultivator can be made a landless sharecropper of the same 2.5 acres, then the annual income of his family will be reduced from 13 quintals to 13—7.5 (50 per cent of production as rent) or 5.5. quintals. This can assure the family, even if the entire income is spent on cereals alone, a per capita per day consumption of 251 grams. Thus, sharecropping, as distinct from ownership of average amount of land, generates a "surplus" of 594—251 or 343 grams per capita per day or a "surplus" of 750 kg. of cereals per sharecropper family of six persons per year, i.e. a surplus of 750 ÷ 2.5 or 300 kg. per acre. Remembering that about 37 per cent of land (or 5 million acres) in West Bengal is under sharecropping, this system generates a surplus of 300 kg x 5 million acre = 1.5 million tonnes.

In the same way, the interest burden at the rate of 60 to 100 per cent or more on the poor cultivators forces them to generate a surplus for the non-agricultural sector. It may be mentioned that as of June 1975, the total outstanding credit from the nationalised commercial banks to the different sectors of the economy of West Bengal as a whole was Rs 10,752 million. Of this amount, the share of the agriculture (excluding plantations) sector, supposed to be the top-most priority sector, mainly for which banks were supposed to have been nationalised, was only Rs 246 million or only 2·2 per cent of the total. This is equivalent to Rs 17.82 per acre. Similar credit from the co-operative banks is now about Rs 340 million or Rs 24.64 per acre. Thus, the organised capital market provided total outstanding loans (short and medium and long-term) of Rs 17·82+24·64 or Rs 42·45 per acre. This is about 15 per cent of the credit need of the peasants even on the basis of present traditional cultivation. The modernised cultivation will generate a need for a credit of Rs 1,000 (term loan or fixed capital loan)+Rs 1,000 (crop loan or working capital loan) making a total of Rs 2,000 per acre. This forced dependence of the peasants today on the unorganised capital market represented by village money lenders is, thus, an additional powerful tool for generating surplus for the nonagricultural sector.

It should further be noted that only a negligible proportion of the organised, formal sector loan to agriculture reaches the rural poor. Thus, in 1973-74, the agricultural labourers, the tenant cultivators, and marginal farmers owning 2.5 acres or less of land—and constituting 78% of the total peasants although owning only 22% of the land—together received only 1% of the total loan advanced by the Cooperative Banks to the agricultural sector. The corresponding share of the term loan advanced by Nationalised Commercial Banks to the above mentioned constituents of the rural poor was only 12 2% [*Economic Review*, 1977-78, Government of West Bengal]

This complex of mechanisms for generating forced surplus or forced saving, the essential base for the type of metropolitan economy the colonialists developed in India to serve their own interests, was the second alternative for solving the growth problem of the metropolitan economy on the basis of low productivity agriculture. And it was this second alternative which was continued in practice, despite talks or legislation to the contrary and perhaps unwillingly, even after independence. If those metropolitan interests, developed during the colonial regime, had not dominated over-all developmental policy in India, then the condition of India's rural areas and agriculture would certainly have been far different from what it is today, and this would have had made possible a far better and healthy urban economy than what exists to-day.

It was on the basis of that strategy that the type of metropolitan, industrial economy that we see even today in the Calcutta metropolis was built. It was this industrial economy that made West Bengal, from a statistical, quantitative point of view, a relatively developed state. Reflection on the quality of this industrial structure, the mechanism of its development, the role it played in the past and is still playing to perpetuate the poverty of the people, leads to the realisation that what has so far been considered as signs of development should be conceived really as remnants of colonial exploitation and plunder of West Bengal's economy.

Because of the lack of realisation of the nature of West Bengal's industrial inheritance, and therefore of the urgent necessity to change the nature of this heritage, the main develomental opportunities before the State were missed. What, however, adds further poignancy to this basic failure was the deprivation of even some short-term developmental benefits that could have accrued to the State had not West Bengal been conceived as a "developed" State. The latter point may be clear from tables 59 and 60. The absolute and relative stagnation and decline of the industrial economy of West Bengal, which means mainly the Calcutta metropolitan economy, may be seen from table 59. Compared to 1963, the share of West Bengal in all-India industrial production had declined by more than 50 per cent in 1975-76. And the volume of industrial production in West Bengal in 1973 was absolutely lower by 14 per cent than what it was even in 1965, while in India as a whole it had increased by 31 per cent during the same period.

Taking India as a whole, growth of output during each of the subsequent three years, viz. 1974-75, 1975-76 and 1976-77 were 2.8%, 6.1%, and 10.00% respectively [*Economic Survey*, 1977-78, Govt. of India]. Thus in 10 years, 1965-66 to 1974-75

TABLE 59

General index of industrial production,
West Bengal and India, 1963—1972
(Base : 1963=100)

	Area	1964	1965	1966	1967	1968	1969	1970	1971	1972	1973
1.	West Bengal	106.6	112.8	104.8	103.1	104.4	99.3	94.3	95.6	97.9	96.9
2.	India	108.6	118 6	117.7	116.7	124.2	133.0	139.3	143 6	153.9	154.8

Source : *Economic Review*, Government of West Bengal (Several years) and *Reserve Bank of India Bulletin* (several issues).

industrial output in India is estimated to have increased by about 34%. In West Bengal, however, income generated from industry, at 1960-61 price, was 3688 miliion in 1965-66 and it *decreased* to Rs 3404 million in 1974-75, denoting a *decline* by nearly 9% in 10 years. The estimated output for 1975-76 is Rs 3552 million, which is still significantly lower than what it was in 1965-66.

This absolute decline in industrial production in West Bengal was associated with a relative and absolute decline in investment. The relevant data for the census sector industry in West Bengal are presented in table 60. During the four years preceding 1966, i.e. during 1961-1965, productive capital investment

TABLE 60

Volume of productive capital invested in census sector industries, West Bengal, 1959/1970

Year	Amount (Rs. million)	Year	Amount (Rs. million)
1954	3 770	1965	12 190
1960	4 350	1966	14 801
1961	4 800	1967	14 540
1962	7 570	1968	13 000
1963	8 710	1969	14 798
1964	10 170	1970	15 046

Source : Annual Survey of Industries, Central Statistical Organisation, Government of India.

in West Bengal increased at an average annual rate of 38.5 per cent ; during the next four years, i.e. during 1966-1970, it increased at an average annual rate of only 0.4 per cent (1970 is the latest year for which full data on investment are available).

Since 1970, only summary data have been made available covering whole of the factory sector, i.e. combining both the census sector and the sample sector, for financial years [April-March]. The relevant information is given below :—

Year	Productive capital (Rs. million)	Fixed capital (Rs. million)
1970-71	15,656	10,491
1971-72	16,663	10,643
1972-73	(Data not published	....
1973-74	15,779	9,547
1974-75	(Comparable data not available)	10,360
1975-76	20,119	11,699

During this period, price level of finished manufactured goods —including capital goods—had increased by nearly 50% ; those of manufactured intermediate products, industrial raw material and wage—constituting the main elements of working capital—had increased by 43% to 74%. Thus, real productive capital base of the factory sector industries in West Bengal actually declined during the whole period.

That the situation since 1970 had not basically improved is clear from the earlier tables and it is even clearer from table 61 giving the number of registered factory workers in the different years. It may be mentioned that 75 per cent of registered factory employment is concentrated in the Calcutta area and that stagnation and decline in employment are more marked in the Calcutta area than in other areas of West Bengal. Table 61 demonstrates that since 1965, on an average, the industry sector became a net generator of absolute unemployment in the state : the volume of such unemployment generated during the four years 1965-1969 amounted to 89,000. During the four years prior to 1965, i.e. 1961-1964, the volume of new employment generated in this sector came to 162,000. This transformation of the metropolitan industry sector from a generator of net new employment at an average annual rate of 5.6 per cent during 1961-1965, however meagre it might have

TABLE 61

Employment in registered factories, West Bengal, 1951-1976

Year	Employment ('000)	Year	Employmet ('000)
1951	652	1968	817
1955	647	1969	791
1958	668	1970	809
1961	781	1971	809
1963	817	1972	831
1965	880	1973	843
1966	840	1974	854
1967	832	1975	839
		1976	835

Source : Chief Inspector of Factories, Government of Wes Bengal.

been compared to the need, to a genarator of net new unemployment, at an average annual rate of 2.5 per cent during 1965-1969, brings to the fore the deep crisis of the Calcutta metropolitan economy. There has been some up-turn in registered factory employment during 1969-1974. The total increase during 1969-1974 came to 63,000 representing an annual rate of growth of 1.6 per cent. The increase, however, was associated with an absolute fall in production by about Rs 120 million. It is evident that such an increase in employment, accompanied by absolute fall in output, cannot be sustained for long, and needs to be taken as a sign of crisis rather than of development. And since 1975 employment started falling again. It went down by 19,000 during 1974-76.

A further manifestation of the crisis of the Calcutta metropolitan economy is evident from the rapidly declining share of

TABLE 62

Share of Eastern Region in all-India exports of engineering goods, 1965/66—1976/77

	Year	Volume of engineering goods exported by All-India	Eastern region	in Rs. million (3) as % of (2)
	(1)	(2)	(3)	(4)
	1965/66	298	194	65.20%
	1966/67	311	141	45.28%
	1967/68	145	120	28.95%
	1968/69	850	358	42.18%
	1969/70	1 064	307	28.89%
	1970/71	1 166	238	20.43%
	1971/72	1 260	256	20.37%
	1972/73	1 505	332	22.09%
	1975/76	4 000	646	16.15%
	1976/77	5 520	1 121	20.30%
Increase to	1965/66 1976/77	5 222	927	17.75%

Source : Engineering Export Promotion Council, Calcutta.

the Eastern region (which practically means, in this context, the Calcutta metropolitan area) in the relatively rapidly rising volume of all-India engineering exports. The relevant data are given in table 62. Even in 1965/66, the Eastern region accounted for more than 65 per cent of total all-India exports of engineering goods ; the corresponding share in 1976-77 was only 20.3 per cent. During the eleven years 1965/66—1976/77 the total volume of engineering exports had increased by Rs 5,222 million, but for the Eastern region it was as low as Rs 927 million or less than even 18 per cent of the total. It may further be mentioned that while in 1951/52, Calcutta port tackled 43 per cent of the goods handled by the major ports in India, the corresponding share for Bombay was less than 34 per cent. In 1973-74, the share of Calcutta port came down to less than 10 per cent. During the period 1951-52 to 1973-74, cargo handled at Calcutta port declined by 35 per cent while that at Bombay increased by 2.6 times, that at Madras by 3.5 times. The pattern of decline of the Calcutta port activity may be seen from table 63.

TABLE 63

Cargo handled at the Calcutta port for export and import 1951-52 to 1975-76

Year	'51-52	'56-57	'61-62	'66-67	'67-68	'68-69
Cargo handled ('000 tonnes)	9,736	8,860	9,302	10,104	8,991	7,965

Year	'69-70	'70-71	'71-72	'72-73	'73-74	'74-75	'75-76
Cargo handled ('000 tonnes)	6,886	6,014	7,359	6,680	6,325	7,536	7,699

Source : Economic Review, Government of West Bengal and Calcutta Port commissioner.

The above tables have not been incorporated in this report to emphasise that while India as a whole is developing at a satisfactory rate, the same is not happening in West Bengal owing to some discriminatory policy. It is well known that India as a whole is passing through a crisis ; the point emphasised here is that within this all-embracing all-India crisis, the situation in West Bengal has become particularly severe owing, on the one hand, to the "developmental burdens" inherited by West Bengal and, on the other hand, to a wrong application of regional development policy by the Centre.

The second developmental alternative followed was to sustain the Calcutta metropolitan economy as inherited from the colonialists. This has meant that despite several good pieces of legislation to the contrary, the rural economic scene of West Bengal continues to be dominated by rack renting, usury and speculative commerce, all thriving on the concentration of land ownership, on the one hand, and lack of any significant employment opportunity outside of agriculture, on the other. And it is these institutions, in the absence of a vigorous programme to increase agricultural productivity, which still perform the crucial role of mobilising forced surplus in the rural areas and transferring them to the metropolitan economy. The dependence of Calcutta's economy on these inequitable and, as we shall see later, anti-productive rural institutions, is at the root of the crisis of both the metropolitan economy and the rural economy.

5.2 The new Technological Possibility

A technological possibility has now arisen, which was not available even ten years back, for introducing a basic change in the low productivity structure of West Bengal's agriculture—the base of the economy. The central points for implementing this possibility are : (i) provision of infrastructure for water management round the year on the basis of ground water Report and conjunctive use of all irrigation sources ; (ii) selection of appropriate seeds and their production and distribution in time ; (iii) supply of adequate doses of manure, fertilizers and pesticides ; and (iv) an effective post-harvest technology including threshing, storage, marketing, etc. Provision of all these prerequisites, particularly in the context of the state of West Bengal, the main hinterland of the Calcutta metropolis, can mean at least a doubling of total agricultural production of West Bengal within five to ten years. Such a possibility makes redundant the current necessity of relying on the present inequitable socio-economic institutions for mobilising forced agricultural surplus, provided that the metropolitan economy takes upon itself, as its main task, the provision of these prerequisites.

With respect to utilising the new technological possibility, there seem to be two different points of view. One emphasises the alleged a-social nature and neutrality to scale of operation of this technological possibility and proposes its introduction within the framework of existing socio-economic institutions. Such an attempt will mean that the majority of the cultivators, who are now victims of the burdens of usury and rack-renting, will not and cannot adopt this modernisation because it will reduce further their already meagre income. It can easily by demonstrated that if capital is to be borrowed at an interest rate of 60 to 100 per cent or more, and if 50 per cent of the gross produce is to be given away as rent to the landlord, and if they are to take resort to distress sale, modern cultivation will reduce the level of income of sharecroppers, and of marginal and small farmers. The small minority of relatively affluent landowners, who have capital resources and are not subject to usury or rack-renting, can be induced to adopt modernisation in agriculture, but only if the rate of return from it is equal to or higher than what they are now accustomed to through money lending, leasing out of land and speculative trading. This will require guaranteeing a high price for agricultural produce which is detrimental to at least 80 per cent of the population, including the overwhelming majority of the peasants, and highly subsidised supply of inputs and unnecessarily heavy investment on infrastructure. This last point needs a little elaboration. This can be done with the help of one example. For efficient water management, the technological basis of modernised agriculture, it will be necessary to have electricity in villages. From the experience of rural electrification in West Bengal, it has been found that the cost of setting up transmission line, including transformers, but excluding the intra-village low tension lines and transformers, comes to more than Rs 50,000 per village. However, less than 5 per cent of the land within its command area (which comes to less than 18 acres per village, having on an average 360 acres of cultivated land) can use this power supply mainly due to the socio-economic constraints mentioned earlier. This means that the overhead cost of power transmission per acre of land using power now comes to Rs 2,780. If this overhead cost is to be recovered in 20 years with a 10 per cent rate of interest through annuity, then the annual payment for this overhead cost will come to Rs 330 per acre. Requirement of consumption of power per acre being of the order of 400 kwh per year, covering the above annuity for transmission overhead alone, will require a charge of Rs 0.82 per unit of power. However, if all the acres of land use that power, then this overhead cost will come down from Rs 2,780 to Rs 140 per acre, and this will mean that the overhead cost per unit of power likely to be consumed per year for irrigating an acre (400 units) will come down from the present level of

Rs 0.82 to the possible level of only Rs 0.04. Assuming that two other elements of cost, viz. oost of direct production of power, and the cost of providing internal transmission lines for connecting the consumer, will be the same under both the circumstances, it may be seen that the total cost of rural power per unit can come down from the present level of Rs 1.00 to only Rs 0.21. This has been calculated on the assumption that the cost for intra-village power connection comes to about Rs 300 per acre, and the annuity on this cost at 10 per cent rate of interest payable in 20 years comes to Rs 39 per acre or less than Rs 0.10 per unit of power. The direct cost of generation of power, at a reasonable level of capacity utilisation, say 75 per cent, has been taken as Rs 0.07 per unit, including cost of maintenance, the wage of operators, and transmission and transportation loss of energy. To-day, when less than 18 acres of land per electrified village utilise power, there is a loss of Rs 0.65 per unit of power, as the present price per unit of power (including duty) comes to only Rs 0.35 (for irrigation purposes). Thus, the total loss per village for supplying it with power comes to about 18 acres × 400 units × Rs 0.65 or Rs 4,680. However, if all the 360 acres in an average village could utilise power, then there would be a profit of Rs 0.35—0.21 or Rs 0.14 per unit of power, or 360 acres × 400 units x Rs 0.14 or Rs 20,160 per village. The contrast between the economics of partial use of power leading to modernisation of only few acres owned mainly by the rich and that of use of power by all the acres of land in the command area of power transmission system should be noted with care.

The actual amount of loss for the public sector is even greater because inducing the richer peasant to adopt modernisation had to include, as we mentioned earlier, guaranteeing a rate of return to which they were accustomed through usury, rack-renting, etc. and this means a huge subsidy for supplying inputs for modernisation, along with guaranteeing high prices for agricultural output. In the case of irrigation water supplied by government, this subsidy often amounted to more than 80 per cent of cost including that required for amortising the capital invested for pumps and tubewells over and above the subsidised price for power (see paragraph below). Taking the amount of total subsidy for power per power-using villages, at the present level of its utilisation, this comes to about Rs 4,680 (from the power-supplying organisation) plus Rs 5,760 (from government-supplying irrigation water) or a subsidy of about Rs 10,000 per power-using village, ultimately from the public exchequer. In addition, there is subsidy on fertilizers, most of which could evidently be used only by the richer peasants and that, too, in those villages with assured irrigation water.

Another aspect of the economics of subsidy should be noted. If we take all the costs into consideration (see reference table J) the present cost of supplying one acre-inch of water by the lift irrigation system comes to about Rs 10 per acre-inch. Despite this, the implied rate charged by the government is as low as only Rs 1.60 per acre-inch, which does not cover even the price of power. The corresponding rate charged by the private suppliers of lift irrigation water, however, is as high as Rs 20 to Rs 40 per acre-inch. And these two rates are interconnected. This subsidy of about 80 per cent of the cost means heavy drainage on public sector resources, making it unable to extend the system at a rapid rate. This inability of the public sector is the objective pre-condition for the ability of the private sector owner of the shallow tube-well, obtained with a loan, in most cases, from a government or nationalised bank, to sell water at such an excessively high price. It has been estimated that had all the peasants purchasing water from lift irrigation sources paid the economic water rate of Rs 10 per acre-inch, then the total cost of the peasants to pay for lift irrigation water supply in West Bengal in 1974 would have been about Rs 210 million. As against this, the peasants pay at least Rs 225 million to private owners and about Rs 24 million to the public sector, i. e. a total of Rs 249 millions or Rs 39 million more than the economic rate. This means that despite the subsidy, or rather because of the subsidy not only does the government lose heavily, weakening the public sector, the peasants also lose heavily. The only beneficiaries in the whole endeavour are the relatively rich private owners of shallow tube-wells, most of whom even do not pay back government or bank loans.

If agriculture were a relatively small economic sector, as is the case with most of the already developed countries, it could be possible to subsidise agriculture in this fashion. In an under-developed country like India, where agriculture still accounts for 75 per cent of material goods production, it is possible to subsidise agriculture only to a very limited extent. Need for subsidy arises in the main, from an attempt to modernise by keeping semi-feudal institution intact. This is one of the main reasons for the extremely limited extent of the rural electrification programme and of the agricultural modernisation programme in West Bengal. Thus, the policy of modernising agriculture, keeping the present social structure intact, is bound to lead to :

(i) an uneconomic, wasteful utilisation of extremely costly overhead facilities including not only power transmission system but also roads, servicing and market centres, etc.

(ii) an extremely limited modernisation leading to a limited use of the vast technological possibilities that have now been opened up before us. This results in very little growth of production compared to what is technologically possible ;

(iii) a rapid accentuation of inter-strata income differences within the village leading to very grave socio-economic-political consequences ;

(iv) extremely limited expansion of the programme in different areas, arising from very limited resources of the state in such an economically poor country like ours, leading to extreme accentuation of regional disparities also leading to very grave economic and political consequences ;

(v) a very limited expansion of the market for industrial goods—capital, intermediate and consumption goods—compared to what is technologically possible ;

(vi) a very limited expansion of supply of agricultural surplus—food and industrial raw materials—because it will still have to depend on "forced saving", compared to what is technologically possible ;

(vii) very limited expansion of productive work opportunity, compared to possibilities, and

(viii) huge import burden, endangering even national independence.

It, thus, appears that the thinking that modern agricultural technology is a-social and can be implemented, at least in such underdeveloped countries like India without a basic change in the existing socio-economic structure is based on a wrong understanding both of the nature of the technology and of the prevailing socio-economic structural constraints on the use of this technology. A continuation of the same wrong thinking, though it appears in a very different garb, is that which portrays the modern technology as suitable for rich cultivators only. The latter implies, either explicitly, or implicitly, that firstly it is possible to cover all or most of the rich farmers in India, keeping the present social structure intact and make a breakthrough in agricultural-industrial production.

Secondly, and this is more dangerous, this modern technology may not be meaningfully used, either actually or in a programatic sense, for ushering in a new and more equitable social order, and then using it fully and successfully in that new socio-economic institutional set up.

It can easily be demonstrated that the modern agricultural technology based on efficient water management and timely supply of other industrial inputs, is neither a-social nor is it particularly suitable for adoption by rich farmers only. This technology can be used with least economic cost and with maximum efficiency only when all the peasants—and the higher the proportion of peasants based on family cultivation the better—in the command area of the provision of those technological facilities, can adopt modernisation. This necessitates an agrarian system based :

(i) not on concentration of land ownership but on as equitable a land distribution as possible ;

(ii) not on rack-renting which reduces the income of sharecroppers by more than half, but on the abolition of the sharecropping system by giving the poor sharecroppers proprietory rights over the land they themselves cultivate mainly with their family labour ;

(iii) not on the present system of usury pushing up the capital cost and hence, all other costs, for the small and marginal farmers, but on making available full credit to all the producers at a low rate of interest from the banking system ;

(iv) not on the present system of speculative trading and *dadan* (advance sale) whereby the poorer majority of peasants are forced to sell their output at a price far lower than the market rate despite their far higher cost of production, but on state-controlled or co-operative-marketing systems ;

(v) not on the present system of starvation wages, and that too for less than half of the year, for landless agricultural labour, but on providing as much land as is possible to them through an egalitarian land distribution system and also by providing them with a living wage all the year round.

Only a programme for building such a socio-economic institutional set up, which has become technologically feasible only recently, and a concerted attempt to implement that programme can generate the social energy to bring about such an economic and technological transformation of West Bengal's rural, agrarian society.

It is the lack of such a transformation in agriculture, involving the major part of the informal (unorganised) sector and also of the entire productive sector, and a lack of involvement of the Calcutta metropolitan economy to bring about such a transformation, that, in the main, ails the metropolitan economy and, along with it, its industrial and trading informal sector. Unless this realisation forms the core of the programme for curing the metropolitan economy of its ailment, any other programme, even if fully implemented, may not only not solve any of the fundamental problems, but in all probability will further aggravate the malady from which the metropolitan economy, and the entire West Bengal economy, is suffering today.

Chapter VI

A PROGRAMME FOR DEVELOPMENT OF THE INFORMAL SECTOR

6.1 Introduction

A programme for development of the informal sector for increasing, and then fully utilising, its productive employment potential involves a restructuring not only of the informal sector, but of the entire economic system. One aspect will have to be freeing the smaller producers from the necessity of depending on the mercy of the large commercial-cum-industrial houses. But this necessarily implies the abolition of one of the major modes of operation for earning huge profits by the large, oligopolistic commercial houses dominating the Calcutta economy, directly or indirectly. It needs to be borne in mind that "doing something good" for the informal sector units may necessarily involve "doing something bad" for the commercial oligarchy and the latter, being very powerful, may, therefore, obstruct, directly or indirectly, any attempt to free the small units from the need for dependence on them.

A second point to be understood in this connection is that, given the existing socio-economic structure, the large units do provide a real service to the smaller units by providing the latter with essential marketing and other allied facilities, although at a very high cost. The present social structure does not provide the small man with any better alternative. It is this that explains the eagerness of the small units to make some contact with the large units for obtaining orders for goods or other similar facilities. They know full well how they are cheated in the matter of price, etc., but it is only this exploitation that can guarantee them a means of livelihood, however meagre it may be. The other alternative provided by the present society to the poor is simple starvation. What is being stated here with regard to small industrial units and the commercial oligarchy in the metropolis, is exactly applicable in the case of small peasants, with a little land or without land, vis-á-vis the landlord, the money lender and the speculative trader, often combined in the same house. If the landless labourer does not get work, even at the pitiable wage of Rs 2 to 3 per day, or if he does not get the right to share-crop the landlord's land even by paying 50 per cent of the gross produce as rent, or if he does not get a loan even with 100 per cent or more interest rate, etc., then the only alternative before him is death, or may be, for a more enterprising few who live nearer the metropolis, an escape to the streets of the metropolis as pavement dwellers (see Annex B).

Despite the various declarations to the contrary, the Government and its allied organisations, including co-operatives, have not been able to provide in the main, any alternative to the overwhelming majority of these informal sector units, in the urban or in the rural areas. The most striking manifestation of this, as we have discussed earlier, is that very few in the informal sector are even aware that there are organisations for providing them any alternative facility, i.e. to most of them the existence of Government as a developmental organisation meant for helping the poor does not have any meaning.

Under these circumstances, neither the small industrial units, particularly the smaller amongst them employing less than ten or less than five persons, including family labour, nor the small peasants either owning no land or owning or share cropping less than 1 or 2 hectares of land, can be expected to organise themselves on their own to become self-reliant by insulating themselves from the need for dependence on the larger commercial industrial units or the landowner money lenders and speculators in the rural areas. Neither is it possible for those in informal sector industry to so improve the level of living of the poorer people (the other market which they serve now) that the latter will demand more and more industrial goods from informal sector industrial units. The removal of poverty of these people, particularly of the overwhelming majority of them now engaged in agriculture in the rural areas, is also integrally linked to a restructuring of the entire industry mix to orient it towards the rural areas for improving productivity in agriculture and that, too, by relying as far as possible on the resources the nation already possesses, and to a basic restructuring of the existing inequitable socio-economic system. This system had some relevance earlier when low productivity in agriculture was in a way inevitable. Then only the institutions characterising the present system could produce the "agricultural surplus" needed to sustain the urban, metropolitan economy and its dominating element, the commercial-industrial oligarchy. But with the emergence of the technological possibility of a dramatic increase in agricultural productivity, the present inequitable socio-economic structure has become redundant, unnecessary and a very big barrier for achieving in practice the technological possibilities of increasing agricultural production.

A correct developmental strategy, in our opinion, should utilise the compulsion of circumstances, the compulsion which affects both the dominating rich and the exploited poor, for developing a programme which will mobilise and organise the poor in the process of implementing the programme itself. With such an organisation, it will be possible for the poor to take conscious and deliberate action to remove the difficulties in the way of further implementation of the programme. This programme should not be based on giving relief or subsidies to the poor—which, any way, cannot be provided on a mass scale—but on helping them to make use of their own resources, which is only partially possible within the present structure of the society. They will then be able to utilise their added economic and organisational strength to move on toward changing the existing structure itself.

It is not possible for a single individual or even for a small group of experts to design such a programme. So what is presented below is merely a suggestion for discussion, both by the learned experts as well as by as many of the local people involved in the field as is possible, so that a viable programme for development may emerge in not too distant a future.

6.2 Suggested outline of a Developmental Programme

By far the most important compulsion of circumstances now operating in India is the need to develop agricultural production rapidly. Whether for fighting galloping inflation or for reducing industrial unrest, or for achieving the political compulsion of removing or at least not further accentuating poverty, or for providing employment or for providing much needed raw materials for industry and cheap and abundant food for the people, or for solving the foreign exchange crisis and becoming self-reliant, the key is far higher agricultural production. This can be achieved through a development strategy centered on the rapid modernisation of agriculture.

A strategy of agricultural development which relies on the few village rich is costly and its capacity to utilise West Bengal's resources is limited. This is gradually leading policy-makers to shift from the strategy based on providing incentives for the rich to develop with some marginal relief for the poor, to an alternative strategy based on utilising total resources—both natural and human—on an areal, spatial basis. "Area-based total development" is becoming an essential feature of developmental strategy.

Another feature of the strategy, which is gradually becoming more and more important, is in effect to change the industry mix by providing added priority to irrigation and hence rural electrification and pumps and tubewells and pipes etc. and to fertilisers, manure, plant protection material and agricultural tools, implements and machinery, the industries required for the development of agriculture and also to mass consumption goods like coarse cloth, etc., demand for which will increase with an increase in income in the agricultural sector.

The third point of this strategy is to change the current use pattern of organised credit. It may be remembered that the big banks in India were nationalised in 1969 with the explicit aim, among others, of providing bank credit to agriculture and small industries.

The development programme for informal sector industry both in the metropolitan as well as in the rural areas will have to be based on four aspects of development: area-based integrated development of agriculture, restructuring the industry mix, restructuring the power use pattern and restructuring credit provision. This is the first essential feature of the recommended developmental programme for informal sector industry.

The second point in this strategy, also applied piecemeal earlier with extremely limited success, is to make informal sector industrial development also an area-based programme. Instead of trying to organise all the existing scattered informal sector units, attempts will have to be made (i) to locate concentrations of such units, (ii) to identify those concentrations which can be easily adapted for supplying inputs to agriculture or inputs to industry meant for agricultural development, and (iii) also to identify those concentrations which can supply cheap consumption goods demanded by the urban and rural poor because demand for such goods is likely to rise at a relatively higher rate.

In the rural area, the comprehensive area development projects or the command area development projects will have to take up the development of small industrial units within the area for servicing industrial installations for agriculture (irrigation and drainage systems, warehousing, etc.), producing spare parts and sometimes simpler equipment and tools and formulations of plant protection chemicals and for producing organic manure and strengthening it with chemical fertiliser or with such raw materials as rock phosphates, etc. These informal sector industrial units will be, so to say, ancillary to informal sector agricultural activity, within the over-all organisation to be set up to manage the area development programmes.

The third aspect of the development strategy is to develop suitable area based organisations with sufficient authority and resources. They will initially be established from the top but are to be replaced by local universal cooperatives or other organisations controlled by the poorer majority within one to three years. Their aim will be to link up informal sector industrial activity as far as is possible with organised informal sector agricultural activity, and also to link up the former with new larger ventures of industrial development meant for agriculture (and other purposes). This will require conscious planning of the proposed big industrial units in the public, private and joint sectors from the stage of project preparation, to take into account the need for, and to plan for development of, ancillary informal sector units located, preferably, in a particular area. Location of all or most of the ancillary units for a particular large factory, in one compact area, will not only facilitate delivery of inputs and outputs, but will also make possible the building up of an effective organisation of the informal sector ancillary units so that collectively they may acquire sufficient strength to bargain with the large unit and with the Government in the matters of pricing, regular order, regular payment, regular supply of scarce raw materials at controlled prices, and also regular credit from the organised sector.

Apart from the 300 comprehensive area development project in West Bengal planned for the Fifth Plan and 700 more for the Sixth Plan, covering 10 million acres in the ten years 1974-1984, it is proposed that about 30 metropolitan CADPs and an additional 70 urban CADPs be set up during the Fifth Plan period.[1] The nucleus of these CADPs will be either existing concentrations of informal sector units with potentials for supplying inputs to agriculture or mass-consumption goods, or the areas where such a concentration can be built up for serving the adjoining agricultural areas. These urban, metropolitan CADPs should have organisational liaison with the rural CADPs on the one hand and the urban metropolitan large agro-industries and other industries on the other. In one sense, they will constitute a higher level in the hierarchy of industrial centres with the lowest—which does not exist now and will have to be established—in every *anchal*, which is a cluster of 8-10 villages, and the highest to be located in the metropolis. This, too, will have to be established because metropolitan industry as it is now constituted cannot become a part of the proposed hierarchy which, in the main will ultimately serve West Bengal's agriculture.

These urban CADP organisations should centre round economic activity and increased productive employment in the specific area ; to this central point will be linked up all other aspects of development—roads, power, health facilities, education and training, etc. This will in a way reverse the existing patterns of metropolitan developmental activity where the provision of these infrastructure facilities is not conceptually linked up, in the programme or in its actual implementation, either with the desired core activity of metropolitan-cum-regional economic

1 Unfortunately, however, state government has sanctioned upto May, 1978, setting up of only 20 rural CADPS.

development or with the different aspects of the physical developments themselves. This suggested reversal can be effected only when it is understood that the fundamental malady in the Calcutta area does not arise from holes in the roads or lack of drinking water or poor drainage or poor transportation facilities or poor education or health services—it arises basically from a sick economic structure that was inherited and which has not been changed so far. The mere provision of some added physical infrastructure, without changing the structural base of the metropolitan economy itself, cannot cure the malady; rather it is likely to accentuate it further by diverting scarce elements (cement, power, organisation, credit etc.) to non-priority sectors.

6.3 The Prospect

This section is based on an estimate, in terms of broad orders of magnitude, of the industrial input requirement of our agriculture in West Bengal.

West Bengal now has 13.8 million acres of net cultivated area and there is little new scope to increase the area further. Rather, with the prospect of agricultural modernisation now becoming visible on our horizon, there should be an attempt, say, 5-10 years hence to have some of these lands covered by forest to restore ecological balance. For the sake of simplicity, it has been assumed that 10.0 million acres will be modernised in ten years starting with 200,000 acres in the first year and then increasing it in a way that by the 10th year 10 million acres are modernised. The immediate industrial implication of the proposed modernisation, based on the data thrown up by the first 13 rural CADP project reports, will be an increase in the industrial input content of agricultural output from the present level of 2-3 per cent to 15-20 per cent. This will mean :

(i) an increase in fertiliser use per acre from 11 kg. of nutrient (N, P_2O_5 and K_2O) per acre per year with 130 per cent cropping intensity in 1976 to 130 kg. of nutrient per acre per year with 250 per cent cropping intensity. Of this 130 kg. it should be possible to supply about 20 kg. from local composts, utilising the entire human, animal farm yard, and household wastes as well as urban wastes —which incidentally, are two times the existing supply of chemical fertiliser—leaving aside 110 kg. per acre, costing about Rs 450 to be supplied by the factory sector ;

(ii) an increase in the use of plant protection material per acre from Rs 10 to about Rs 150 per acre per year.

The above two requirements will mean that the chemical industry will have to supply an additional Rs 450× 200,000 acres worth of chemical fertilizer+Rs 150× 200,000 acres of plant protection material or Rs 120 million worth of goods per year for the project areas in the initial year, to be increased to Rs 6,000 million per year in 1985 when the proposed 10 million acres are to be modernised. This likely demand by 1985 (including 1.10 million tonnes of nutrient from the factory sector) may be contrasted with the present supply of Rs 500 million worth of such goods per year for the agriculture sector in West Bengal as a whole ; and West Bengal industries as such play an insignificant role in supplying even this meagre amount.

(iii) an increase in the use of power from the present West Bengal average of about 5 units per year per acre to about 400 units per year per acre in 1985 or a total of at least 4000 million units per year. This will require a firm capacity of at least 670 MW or an installed capacity of at least 830 MW. The initial 200,000 acres of compact modernised blocks will require at least 80 million units. In 1976-77 irrigation for West Bengal as a whole got only 68.2 million units constituting only 1.2 per cent of the total power consumed in West Bengal as a whole. This additional power generating capacity will require an investment of Rs 2,000 million ; additional investment requirement for installing the connection to the new irrigation tube wells will be at the rate of Rs 400 per acre in as yet non-electrified villages and Rs 230 per acre in the already electrified villages.

(iv) calculating in terms of what are popularly called shallow tube wells with a 5 HP pump capable of irrigating, with proper water management and proper crop comination channels, etc., about net 10 acres throughout the year, with a life of less than 10 years, this modernisation programme will require a production capacity of 0.1 million sets of shallow tube wells per annum with an output value of Rs 500 million per year.

(v) Assuming that 75 per cent of the land (or 7·5 million acres) will use hand sprayers for spraying plant protection material, that each such sprayer can manage 10 acres and that it has a life of seven years, then there will have to be a production capacity of 75,000/- per year with an output value of Rs400 × 75,000 or Rs 30 million per year.

(vi) Assuming that the remaining 25 per cent of the land will use power sprayers, each with a capacity of 50 acres and a life of three years, immediate annual production capacity will have to be for 5,000 units to be raised to 10,000 units from the third year with an ultimate output value of Rs 1,000 × 10,000 or Rs 10 million per year.

(vii) Assuming that one combined power thresher for wheat and paddy can tackle the output of 100 acres and that each has a life of seven years, then there should be a production capacity of 10,000 units per annum with an output value of Rs 1800 × 10,000 or Rs 18 million per year.

(viii) Assuming that with about 2.5 crops per year, there will be need, after fully using local bullock and human power, for 15 per cent of the land (or 1.5 million acres) to be ploughed by power tillers and another 15 per cent by tractors, there should be a production capacity for 2,000 tractors, each tackling net 100 acres, and 10,000 power tillers per year, each with a capacity of 20 acres and with a life of seven years. Total value of output will be Rs 62,000 × 2,000 + Rs 22,000 × 10,000 or Rs 344 millions per year.

(ix) In addition, there will be a requirement for smaller

implements like MB ploughs, seed drills, wheel hoes, etc. Compared to the requirement of four pairs of bullocks per day per acre with ordinary ploughs, the MB ploughs can reduce the requirement of bullock power by 50 per cent. Each of these ploughs will cost Rs 30, which is the same as ordinary ploughs, and will last for seven years. Even if 50 per cent of the land is tilled with MB ploughs, then the annual requirement will be of the order of 0.1 million with an output value of Rs 3 million. The requirement of seed drills, one each for 15 acres and with seven years' life, will be 35,000 per year with value of Rs 3.5 million. The magnitude of requirement of wheel hoes will be the same and its annual value will be Rs 1.8 million.

Summarising the requirements of industrial inputs stated above (and this does not include the requirements of stores, cold storage, transport and the like) we may see that the implication of giving top priority to elimination of poverty and hence to agriculture—because in the context of our country, it is agriculture which produces the wherewithal to fight poverty—is, among other things, that industry should by 1985 be able to supply the following annual inputs to agriculture for West Bengal alone :

(1) Chemical goods worth Rs 6,000 million per year.

(2) At least 4,000 million Kwh of power worth Rs 1,280 million per year at the present price rate for power.

(3) Engineering goods worth :

(a) Rs 500 million for tubewells and pumps ;

(b) Rs 40 million for sprayers ;

(c) Rs 18 million for threshers ;

(d) Rs 344 million for tractors and tillers ;

(e) Rs 2 million for MB ploughs, wheel hoes and seed drills

Total Rs 904 million of engineering goods per year.

Only the three items noted above make a total annual requirement of industrial goods for agriculture worth Rs 8,184 million. In addition, there will be a requirement for heavy capital goods such as power plants, factories for producing those inputs, transmission towers, and the like. Even if we spread these heavy capital investments over ten years, annual investment goods to be produced on this count will have to be of the order of Rs 1,500 million.

At the present level of productivity and of input and labour use, working capital need per acre is about Rs 300, of which, now about Rs 20 are provided by the commercial banks (most of which in term loan) and Rs 25 by the cooperative banks, leaving Rs 255, or 85 per cent of the credit requirement to be supplied by the village money lender often at an interest rate exceeding 100 per cent per annum. Modernised agriculture will need working capital of the order of Rs 1,000 per acre for paying for the inputs and for labour (including maintenance of family labour). This is in addition to Rs 1,000 of direct fixed capital with an average life span of 10 years. This level of credit cannot be supplied by the village money lender and, what is more important, it will not be worthwhile for the peasants to modernise with borrowed capital bearing an interest rate of 50 to 100 per cent or more. This credit will have to be supplied by the banks. The order of magnitude of this credit requirement for 10 million acres by 1985 will be Rs 10,000 million as working capital and 1,000 millon as direct fixed capital (renewing 10 per cent of the direct fixed capital every year) or a total of Rs 11,000 million per year. This is higher than the total outstanding credit of Rs 10,752 million from the commercial banks to West Bengal as a whole as of June 1975, and it is nearly 200 times the total credit now being provided to West Bengal agriculture by the combined effort of the commercial and cooperative bank together !

The compulsion of circumstances, noted earlier, is pushing us inexorably towards the pattern of production and of credit visualised above. The significance of this pattern may be understood from the facts that our state of West Bengal, despite its designation as a relatively advanced industrial state of India, scarcely produces any of these goods now, though it does produce a lot of other industrial goods ; and that of the total outstanding credit from commercial banks to West Bengal, only 2.2% goes to the agricultural sector now.

Our scarce resources should not be frittered away on relatively non-priority items ; and the other development programmes should be designed to become a positive force to push toward a total modernisation of agriculture based on a restructuring of existing inequitable and anti-productive socio-economic institutions, and a basic change in the industry mix, the power supply mix, and the structure of credit availability. This can be achieved only by a self reliant, militant organisation of the rural and urban poor.

The programme for creating, and then using, the productive employment potential in the Calcutta area informal sector, will, thus, have to be designed as an integral part of the above prospect. On the fulfilment of the above prospect depends elimination of underemployment from agriculture, the dominant form of unemployment in India, and creation of a real and massive agricultural surplus for sustained long-term developmental activity, which is necessary to generate massive new employment in the non-agricultural sector. The informal sector in the Calcutta metropolis can be made to stand on its feet and play a significant role if it can be integrated into such a prospect.

Annexure—A

A note on the design for the survey of slum Induseries in the Calcutta area

Purpose : To find out the tasks required to be undertaken to realise in practice the employment potential of informal sector industries in general and Calcutta area slum industries in particutar.

Methodology : As the main purpose was qualitative rather than quantitative, it was decided that instead of random sample, it would be better to make a purposive selection of few typical slum areas with concentration of industrial units in such a way that one or more slums were covered from most of the zones in the Calcutta metropolitan centre, dominated you Calcutta city proper. Accordingly, 11 survey zones were selected as noted below. From amongst these we identified one or more geographical clusters in which more or less complete lists of the units were prepared. These units were then covered through the survey.

The Calcutta metrpolitan core was divided into 11 survey zones as noted below :

Serial No	Name of survey zones
1.	Howrah city North
2.	Howrah city Central
3.	Howrah city South
4.	Cossipore, Baranagar, Paikpara, Datta Bagan (northern suburb of Calcutta)
5.	Kidderpore, Matiaburuz, Santoshpore (South-West Calcutta)
6.	Chetla (South-Central Calcutta)
7.	Baithakkhana, Rajabagan, Narikeldanga, Fulbagan (Central Calcutta)
8.	Beliaghata, Manicktola, Bagmari, (North-East Calcutta)
9.	Entally-Park Circus (Central-East Calcutta)

10. Jorabagan, Rambagan, Kumartolly, Chorbagan (North-West Calcutta)

11. Tangra-Tiljala (East Calcutta)

After listing the units, these were divided into 56 industry types which were then re-grouped into 12 industry groups. The pattern may be clear from the industry code list below.

Name of the industry group	Name of the industry type	Code
01 Food and tobacco	(a) Chaki	011
	(b) Rice mills	012
	(c) Dal mills	013
	(d) Flour mills	014
	(e) Bhuja jalpan shops	015
	(f) Sugar candy and ice cream	016
	(g) Mustard oil	017
	(h) Pickles, jelly, bakery, canned fruits	018
	(i) Sweet confectionery	019
	(j) Bidi making	0110
	(k) Other tobacco products	0111
	(l) Others	0112
02 Textiles	(a) Sari, cloth printing and embroidery	021
	(b) Textile weaving	022
	(c) Rope making	023
	(d) Hosiery dyeing, hosiery lace, allied products	024
	(e) Others	025
03 Wood	(a) Wooden furniture, Wooden accessories, wooden frames	031
	(b) Sawmills, wood packing boxes	032
	(c) Umbrella sticks	033
	(d) Foot wear (wooden)	034
	(e) Bamboo products	035
	(f) Jute mill bobbins and looms	036
	(g) Wooden toys, sports, wooden spoons, etc.	037
	(h) Others	038

Name of the industry group	Name of the industry type	Code
·04 Paper	(a) Card board boxes, card board tubes, card board products, paper bags, paper boxes	041
·05 Printing	(a) Book binding, printing presses	051
·06 Leather	(a) Shoe making, leather goods, tube-well washers, etc.	061
·07 Rubber	(a) Rubber products	071
·08 Chemicals	(a) Acid	081
	(b) Medicine manufacturing	082
	(c) Soap making	083
	(d) Napthelene, sealing wax, wax, celluloid comb, bottle manufacturing	084
	(e) Paints	085
	(f) Incense-sticks	086
	(g) Plastic toys, ink, stamp pads, cosmetics	087
	(h) Others	088
·09 Non-metalic mineral products	(a) Building materials	091
	(b) Potteries, image, clay-model makers	092
	(c) Glass ampules, scientific glass apparatus	093
	(d) Others	094
10 Metal products (excluding machinery)	(a) Wire netting	101
	(b) Conduit pipes	102
	(c) Wire drawing, wire nails, belts	103
	(d) Tin boxes, tin toys	104
	(e) Household utensils	105
	(f) Collapsible gates, grills, windows, Steel rails	106
	(g) Steel almirahs, cabinets	107
	(h) Welding and metal products, iron foundry	108

Name of the industry group	Name of the industry type	Code
	(i) General engineering	109
	(j) Hoop iron	1010
	(k) Biscuit-making machinery, tablet machines,	10
	Power presses	1011
	(l) Razors, scissors, tongue scrapers, spades	1012
	(m) Electro-plating, galvanising	1013
	(n) Canteen equipment	1014
	(o) Agricultural tool manufacturing and repairing	1015
	(p) Others	1316
11. Machinery	(a) Ceramic insulators, electrical goods	111
	(b) Motor parts, tools, cardboard machinery manufacture	112
	(c) Engineering goods machinery,	113
	(d) Shades of fluorescent lamps	114
	(e) Bobbin pins	115
	(f) Cycle parts, motor parts, locomotive machinery spare parts, ancillary parts	116
	(g) Dies	117
	(h) Bobbin making and rickshaw coach making	118
	(i) Others	119
12 Miscellaneous	(a) Jewellery shops, conchshell products	121
	(b) Musical instruments	122
	(c) Photo-frames, watch repairing, fountain pen, optical frames	123
	(d) Kerosene lamps, washer mantle of Hanzaq, hospital furnishings	124
	(e) Mosaic tiles, brick dust	125
	(f) Distilled water	126

Name of the industry groop	Name of the industry type	Code
	(g) Straw cutting	127
	(h) Others	128

Along with preparing the list of a units, a first draft of the survey schedule was prepared and a pilot survey was conducted for pre-testing the schedule, as well as for providing direct field training in the industry survey to the group of social workers—attached to CUSCON, CMPO, and CMDA—who were to conduct the survey.

After finishing the survey schedule, a copy of which appears at the end of this note, a detailed written instruction was provided to the investigators and several discussion meetings-cum-training classes were held.

Survey schedules were scrutinised by senior staff, coded according to a code list prepared earlier, and then the information was transferred to punched cards and fed to a unit record machine which provided us with basic data sheet. Final tables were prepared with the help of this basic data sheet.

TYPE STUDY OF INDUSTRIAL UNITS IN CMD SLUM AREAS, 1973

CMPO-CMDA-CUSCON-DIR. OF C & SSI-SPB

BLOCK-I : Identification

Slum Identity	Industry Type
A.	B.

C. Schedule No ____________________

D. Name of Investigator ____________________

E. Name of the Unit/Owner ____________________

F. Factory Address ____________________

____

G. Name and status of informant ____________________

H. Type of legal organisation ____________________

I. Is registered ? (a) as SSI ____________________

(b) under Factories Act ____________________

J. Area of the workshop : Covered ______________ sq. ft.
Open ______________ sq. ft.

K. Type of structure ____________________

L. Is the workship used also for residential purpose ? ____

____

BLOCK II : Employment

A. No. of days the factory worked during last one year (November, 1972—October, 1973) ____________________

B. No. of shifts per day the factory normally works

C. Total employment in the shift with maximum employment ____________

D. Total employment possible in that shift if there is no constraint in raw material, working capital or market. ____________

E. Average daily employment by season :

Season	Total daily employed		No. of hours worked		Monthly emolument per wage Labour	Remarks if any
	Family Labour	Wage Labour	Family Labour	Wage Labour		
a) busy Season — to —						
b) Slack Season — to—						

F. No. of workers residing

Within the bustee	Within one mile	More than one mile	Total

G. Educational Level of Workers

Level	Family Labour	Wage Labour
a) Illiterate		
b) Upto Class V		
c) V to Class X		
d) S. F. & above		
e) Others		
Total		

H. Locational motivation :—

A)

B)

C)

BLOCK III : Capital

A. Stock of Tools and Machinery :

Type	Year of Purchase	Purchase price	Indian or Foreign
i)			
ii)			
iii)			
iv)			
v)			
vi) Others			
Total			

B. Already Planned to Purchase additional Tools & Machinery

Type	Price	Indian or Foreign
i)		
ii)		
iii)		
iv)		
Others		

C. Total connected H. P. of the installed Machines ______

D. Land and Building : Present value ______ ____
Monthly rent ______ ____

E. Total Working Capital ______ ____

F. Source of Capital : Inherited %
Own savings % Loan %

G. Source of Loan

Source	Amount borrowed during the year ending Oct.'73	Amount outstanding on 31st Oct. 1973	Rate of Interest per year	Security
i) Bank				
ii) Government				
iii) Friends/ relatives				
iv) Mahajans*				
v) Others				
Total				

* Private money lender.

BLOCK IV : Capacity and production.

A. Production and export

Item of manufacture	Annual installed capacity (per shift) Quantity	Actual Production during year ending October, 1973.		Exported during year ending October, 1973.	
		Quantity	Value	Quantity	Value
i)					
ii)					
iii)					
iv)					
v)					
vi)					
vii)					
Total					

B. Input use

Item of input	Annual requirement based on one shift Capacity (Quantity)	Actual consumption during year ending October, 1973		Quantity imported during yearending October, 1973.
		Quantity	Price	
i)				
ii)				
iii)				
iv)				
v)				
vi)				
vii) Others				
Total :				

BLOCK V : Marketing

Item	Amount (Rs.) sold & purchased during year ending Oct. '1973 to/from							
	Whole seller	Retailer	Consumer	Dadandar	Parent firm	Total Sale/ purchase	Against cash	Against credit
1. Sale of output								
2. Purchase of input								

BLOCK VI : Difficulties & their solutions.

A. Experience of getting credit from :

(a) Bank................................

....

(b) Government.....................

....

(c) Others..............................

....

B. Experience of getting raw material from :

(a) Open market..........................

....

(b) Government..........................

....

(c) Others..............................

....

C. Experience of selling finished goods in :

(a) Open market ____________________

(b) Government ____________________

(c) Others ____________________

D. Experience of Labour management :

(a) Lack of training :

(b) Lack of discipline :

(c) Non availability of skilled labour :

(d)____________________

E. Specific advantage or disadvantage of the existing location :—

F. Other difficulties & suggestions :

Signature of scrutinizer with date.	Signature of Investigating Officer with date.

ANNEXURE—B.

ECONOMIC ACTIVITY OF PAVEMENT DWELLERS

A survey of pavement dwellers, the most informal amongst the informal sector activities, was conducted by the same band of social workers who conducted the field survey on slum industries, under the very able guidance of Dr Sudhendu Mukherjee, formerly Urban Sociologist of CMPO and now with the CMDA.

According to the 1971 census, there was a houseless population of 50,342 in Calcutta. The sample for this survey consisted of 10,000 families with 34,316 persons, 55 per cent of whom were males. This nearly balanced sex ratio reflects the fact that 81 per cent of them lived with families. What is striking is the fact that 31.6 per cent of these people, or 10,841 persons, were earners, and they made it possible to provide a monthly per capita income of Rs. 23.35 which, incidentally, was certainly above that provided to the bottom 20 per cent of the population.

TABLE 64

Occupation pattern of the 10,841 earners amongst the 34,316 pavement dwellers, Calcutta city, 1971

Nature of occupation	No. of earners	Percentage distribution
(1)	(2)	(3)
1. Push cart workers	706	6.5
2. Rickshaw pullers	794	7.3
3. Rag pickers	521	4.8
4. Vegetable sellers	392	3.6
5. Maid servants	458	4.2
6. Other regular day labour	933	8.6
7. Casual day labour	2 499	23.4
8. On charity/begging	2 399	22.0
9. Others	1 794	16.5
Total	10 841	100.0

Source : Census of India, 1971

Of the 10,841 earners, nearly 34 per cent were in regular employment and another 28 per cent were in casual employment. They performed very useful services particularly to the other informal sector activities. The remaining 38 per cent depended on various other sources of income including begging and charity. The distribution of these earners by the nature of their occupation is shown in table 64.

Table 65 gives the distribution of these earners by the level of their income. It may be seen from the table that 84 per cent of the earners had an income of more than Rs. 20 per month and more than 50 per cent had an income of more than Rs. 60 per month.

TABLE 65

Distribution of the earner pavement dwellers by the level of their monthly income, Calcutta city, 1974

Monthly income level per earner	No. of earners	Percentage distribution
(1)	(2)	(3)
Uncertain	385	3.4
Less than Rs. 10	360	3.3
Rs. 10—20	1 034	9.5
20—40	1 793	16.5
40—60	1 950	18.7
60—80	1 213	11.1
80—100	1 592	14.6
100—120	1 068	9.8
120—140	592	5.4
140—160	254	2.3
160—180	167	1.5
180—200	155	1.4
200+	278	2.5
Total	10 841	100.0

The data relating to the strata of the population from which the pavement dwellers come throw considerable light on the nature of our economy itself. Thus nearly 49 per cent of the migrant pavement dwellers were agricultural labourers who came to the city because of lack of work in the agricultural sector and who continued to stay because the level of earnings in the city even as a pavement dweller was perhaps not worse than what it was in the area from where they hailed. The average earning per agricultural worker is about Rs. 600 per year or Rs. 50 per month. This average, like most averages, hides wide variations around that average. In the wide saline tract lying to the south of the Calcutta area in general and in the Sunderban areas in particular, often this level is less than Rs. 30 per month on an average. The situation is similar in drought prone areas in Purulia and parts of Bankura and Midnapore. The situation is often worse in the neighbouring. state of Bihar. The other migrant pavement dwellers, just like migrant agricultural labourers, came to the city predominantly because of the poverty in the rural area. This may be seen from table 66.

TABLE 66

Percentage distribution of the pavement dwellers by the cause of their migration

Cause of migration	Economic	Political	Social	others	Total
Percentage of pavement dwellers	86.7	5.3	3.3	4.7	100.0

One more finding from the Survey Report written by Dr Sudhendu Mukherjee should be quoted. This concerns the food "habit" of the respondents. On being asked during the survey how many times they took food the previous day, 156 families (1.6 per cent) replied that they had not taken any food at all and 3,646 families (36.5 per cent) replied that they could get food only once in the whole day. The remaining 62 per cent of the families appeared to have eaten at least twice the previous day. They were, however, not asked about the quantity and, particularly, the quality of food they took. But what is striking is the fact that while only 30 per cent of the population are above the poverty line, i.e. capable of getting at least two square meals a day, the proportion amongst pavement dwellers of such persons appears to be higher. This brings to the fore that the level of living of the pavement dwellers is perhaps somewhat better than the level of living of the overwhelming majority of the population, particularly in the rural areas. And so long as the condition of the rural poor is not markedly better than the prospects of pavement dwelling in the Calcutta city, pavement dwellers will remain and their number will increase.

There will be another appendix or Comprenensive Area Development Projects West Bengal.